Start With The Breadsticks

Principles on How To Not Suck:
a book written for the radical pilgrimage

TO DEAN,

Zac Sweat

Dear:
We still gotta
find time 2 play
some pickle ball!

—Wes—

"I did not write,
but I wrote the
forward!"

Book cover and typesetting by: HMDpublishing

Contents

For James and William

two souls and two paths taken in life that taught so many lessons

Foreword

The year was 1995 and we were thirteen years old. I vividly remember my parents' unfinished basement, wooden stairs leading down into my dad's office/ tool workshop on one side and a home made music/ recording studio on the other. My parents had allowed my best friend Zac and I to use the empty space in any way we wanted. Zac and I decided to create and build a music/ jam area. We both played guitar but Zac was on the hunt to get a drum kit and play like his favorite drummer at the time, Adrian Young, from the band No Doubt.

Zac's parents were working on getting him a drum kit, but Zac couldn't wait and asked my parents if he could use old paint cans in the basement in the meantime to construct and build a makeshift temporary drum set. After carefully selecting several paint cans with the right auditory projection, he had compiled a pretty damn solid 5-piece kit out of household items. We were ready to jam! We spent hours in that basement, listening to music, laughing, telling jokes, and talking about life. We rode bikes together during the summer, buried a time capsule of our favorite guitar hero magazine, some guitar picks and a cassette tape of a song we recorded called "Golden Boy. Each weekend was an adventure filled with excitement and laughter. We would join forces, dream, envision, create, and live. Zac's friendship and presence blessed my life back then in unspeakable ways and it is beyond surreal to have him in my life again after twenty-four years apart.

Zac and I parted ways in freshman year of high school, gravitating towards different friend groups and slowly losing touch over the years. After leading separate lives and each going on our journeys of growth and development, Zac has entered back into my life through what I believe to be divine intervention. We have reconnected and once again dreamed, envisioned, and manifested, this time bringing into existence an Experiential Therapeutic Youth Center, which provides sacred space for youth to get support on their journey of growth and for this I am beyond grateful and indebted to Zac.

Zac's energy and presence has always held a special place in my heart. Ever since I have known Zac he has led with his heart and soul. Being around him, I have always felt free, energized, and charged to dream, laugh, and love. Zac has been on his own miraculous growth journey of development and has chosen to share his personal journey with others to help them do the same. Much like that thirteen year old kid who let his energy lead him to start and pursue his dreams without waiting for the perfect time or the perfect tools, Zac continues to bring a free spirit energy of engagement and pedal to the metal attitude to holistic growth.

Zac puts his heart and soul into his healing, coaching, and counseling of clients and families and brings truth, knowledge, guidance, and sacred space to all he does. In the following pages, Zac lays out clearly a universal truth of how to move towards your true potential and let go of anything that is not serving your greatest good and growth. With deep insight, structure, and strategy, Zac provides tools, guidance and wisdom. He blends and weaves together elements of self-growth, Buddhist psychology, depth psychotherapy, bodymind connection, and discipline/

structure to create a gut punch tool kit of empowerment for the individual.

This book, if read and engaged with properly, can absolutely shift your life toward light, beauty, and prosperity. Zacs' gifts are far too lengthy to list in depth, but his heart and soul are in this book. Zac continues to grow, learn, strengthen, and challenge himself each day, but what I admire most is his continued and relentless desire to help teach, push, and guide others toward their true potential. Zac is a warrior spirit with only one agenda in this life, which is to help others connect to their true selves and to live lives of freedom and passion.

Zac's words, guidance, and connection have brought beauty, strength, and positive impact to my life in a multitude of ways. *Start with the Breadsticks* is a heartfelt, direct, clear, and honest guide for anyone wishing to grow, strengthen, and reconnect with the unlimited potentiality of their soul's voice!

Weston J. Robins, LPC

Acknowledgements

Although cliché in nature, I must first and foremost thank my mother Connie. She has been one of the most understanding, supportive women I have in my life. She has been a great mother to me and my siblings. Come to think of it, there isn't one bad thing I could say about her. No matter what place I have been at in my life she has always just sat with me through it and always stated her favorite catch phrase, "As long as you're happy," and maybe she didn't ever know, but I actually wasn't in all the years. I have stayed in the space of no direction, meaning, or purpose. I thought I was happy, but no matter what she was always there with an understanding outlook on the life that was before me. Now, maybe on the inside she wanted to shake me and yell, "WAKE UP YOU BASTARD!" But, she didn't, and for that I love her. It's not for someone to do the work for you. And it's not up to YOU to tell a person when that time is, all you can do is encourage and exude love to them, and that's exactly what she did. Thanks, Mom.

For my Dad, Dave. Always giving it to me straight, no bullshit, no filter, no sugar on top. Just facts. And I find myself in these last few years observing that in me. Direct in nature but backed with love. Some people see it as being an asshole, and I can honestly admit, yeah, I can see that, but when you're not used to speaking your own truth it's hard to take others when they fully express it. Thanks pops.

My sister, Nicole, has always had my back, no questions asked. Thanks for that. Our relationship has grown over these past few years when we both decided to live out our own truths. Leaving the bullshit behind, she inspires me.

My friend, June Dillinger. Oh June...you have played such a major role in my life. I know you know that, but I am not sure you know how big your role actually was and still is. June lives with grace, determination, full authenticity, and vigor. My time by her side as a friend in Hawaii will always be remembered, cherished and looked upon as some of the most influential, significant, loving times of my life.

And my friend, Sean. Sean was my road dog, mentor, and close friend during my time in Hawaii, where most of this book was written and inspired from. He was one of the few people that would check me when needed. He always looked out for my greatest good, inspiring me to push myself to the limits, and then even further. He was always there whenever needed no questions asked. Thank you, Sean.

Shout out to Omar Sungar, my vegan friend. One of the hardest working motherfuckers on this planet. Your time is now brother. Thank you for always being authentic, raw, and funny as hell. I always told you your energy was at a level that most people would never understand, and I still mean that, thank you for allowing that energy to inspire me.

Next, I would like to thank Wes Robins. Wes has been one of the greatest coaches, mentors, and friends to me. Knowing each other since the 6th grade, it has been a hell of a trip. Even though we lost connection for sometime in our lives, going through our own dark night of the soul, we have now reconnected and we entered back into each other's lives, that I believe to be, at a divine time. The stars have aligned and the universe opened up to us and we have been on a crazy motherfucking rollercoaster in the past few months I have been home from Hawaii. He has encouraged me in ways that have opened my mind to an entirely different world. I have seen myself and others in a different light. I look up to him (but don't tell him I said that). He is beyond a great father, husband, brother, teacher, mentor, healer, trickster, and shaman. He has truly blessed my life and has helped me to finish this book and make it what it is. For that I am more than a grateful brother.

To all the online and academic mentors I have taken into my life, I say thank you. Without your powerful words guiding me daily, I am not sure where I would be. Without the constant seeds of motivation, power, capability, relentless determination, and belief in self I could not have continued the forward progression that has gotten me to where I am today.

From the minds of people like: Abraham Hicks, Bob Proctor, Jordan Peterson, Jim Rohn, Terrence Mckenna, Alan Watts, Jack Canfield, Tony Robbins, Robin Sharma, Napoleon Hill, Dan Pena, Les Brown, Dr. Myles Monroe, Tom Bilyeu, Eric Thomas, Mel Robins, Ram Dass, Simon Sinek, Sadghuru, and many more I have been moved to take massive action with my life and for that I am beyond humbled and grateful. I highly encourage each of you reading this to tap into the minds of these great leaders by purchasing their books, listening to their lectures, and applying their infinite wisdom to your life. I consider myself a lifelong student and these have been some of my greatest teachers and mentors, whether they know it or not.

And thank you to the youth and young adults I have the absolute honor and pleasure of sitting and sometimes walking beside during their growth and development. You guys have taught me more than you know.

For anyone I have crossed paths with during this time here on earth, thank you. I consider all interactions in my past life and my future to be opportunities for growth and expansion.

For anyone I might have left out, I have not done this with any intention. I have had so many beautiful connections in my life, and I type this I feel as abundant as ever. I cannot believe life has taken me to this point. I am thankful everyday and I try my best to not let one day pass without saying thank you.

I am grateful daily.

Preface

I suck...

OK...Wait, wait, wait.....pump the brakes... at least.... I used to.

I did! And I'm cool with it. I can honestly and openly admit this to you and myself. I have accepted it. And it was in that acceptance of myself when I realized there lied within, some true power. First, by recognizing it. Secondly, by wanting to do something about it. I wanted to figure out...

How to Not Suck.

And look, this may be a harsh way to come at this whole life thing, but I firmly believe that we all need a heavy dose of this type of medicine. A swift kick in the ass if you will. What good is it going to do your highest self by continuing to deny that you don't suck in some (if not all) departments of life. I sucked in multiple departments. Admitting this truly opens some amazing space within you for something very empowering and magical to enter your life and could alter your current course.

These.

Are.

Facts.

These are my philosophies. My principles. These are my truths. These are the tools that I used to heal myself. These are the tools I still use and apply. I once read (somewhere) that you cannot own a truth, but you can surely live by them and share them with the world. You might not agree with the principles I share in this book and that's totally cool. But what I do ask of you is that you read through this authentic material with an open heart and an open mind.

I have been called to be of service, not only to myself but to others. I do *my* part by sharing the experiences, ideas, philosophies, principles and truths that has put me on the path I am on today.

This path that not only has led me to you but has had such a major impact on the way I live my life. This path consists of me sharing my light with others. We are all lightworkers. We have all been placed here to be of service to one another and to share, learn, and grow together. This book and the message I share is based on that premise.

I promise I am not telling you things that you don't already know, but maybe have been long forgotten during your own personal journey. I am only reminding and reinforcing what you already know to be true. Allow yourself to understand that. The knowledge has always been there. Again, it might have been diluted down from all the years of your conditioning that has taken place. Mix that notion and throw in the many distractions that this current world of ours offers and this knowledge can easily be pushed down to a place where it no longer sees the light. Your light.

So, let's uncover this knowledge that rests inside of you. Let's tap back into your powerful potential. Let's focus on reuniting with our true nature.

Life is challenging, I get it. We all experience it. So why not experience it at our best? Why not live our days in a joyful state and immersed in our own flow? Please stop and think for a moment why you *wouldn't* want to live this way, doesn't make sense, does it?

Wanting to do better, to be better...its ok to desire that. It's our birthright to thrive, to love, to grow, to learn, to experience, and to be able to live in an abundant and fulfilling world with the people we care about.

Do not let anyone tell you differently. You are a creator. You are a badass. You have such an ability to create a magnificent existence for yourself. So many of us walk around, head down, tiptoeing through life as if we have more than one shot at this thing. We don't! It's one life, baby. So why not make some noise? Why not fully express yourself the way you would like to? Why not strive to reach our fullest potential? So at some point you have to ask yourself, "Am I doing the very best I can?" "Am I being all that I am capable of becoming?" And if the honest, most sincere answer is no, then why not start working in a direction that will not only benefit you, but everyone you encounter. Working on ourselves is the absolute best thing we can do. Treating yourself in the best possible way will show up in every aspect of your life. It starts with you and spreads from there. Let me remind you again, you are a lightworker. You are meant to shine, illuminate, and help others do the same. I suppose that's where my inspiration comes from. This is my way of shining. Sharing my talents, being of service to others and myself. Everybody wins.

Throughout this book are many lessons, learning opportunities, and blessings formulated into principles. And yes, although the title is a little strong, and some would say extreme, I made it that way for a reason, and the tone used throughout this book is one stemming from a position of love, just know that. Although I might drop some f- bombs and carry an in-your-face approach at times, just know that it does come from the sincerest, most authentic place in my heart. Seriously, this book expresses what some of us just might need to hear. Consider it a gentle kick-in-the-ass, if you will.

Trust me when I say this book first addresses me. Oh yeah, I needed that kick in the ass. These principles come from a place of firsthand experience, and I side with the notion that, why not share this for other people? Why not allow others to learn from your own learning opportunities? Because the things I speak about in this book, you're not going to find within the classrooms at a trade school, community college, or university and courses that they offer.

This is my offering to you. Some good ol' self-education. I pride myself on self-educating for almost the last three years of this beautiful journey of personal development and discovery. We should always be educating ourselves in some way. Learning, growing, and allowing that information to lead us down a path that we can be proud of. But not just learning it, but really applying it. That is going to be the key. Application. We can read and read all day long, but if we are not taking the action and application needed to use these principles and benefit from their teachings then what's the use?

And look, I am humble enough to put my shit out there. I really don't mind. There have been so many before me that have done the same thing. I took note of all the people that I have followed along this self-discovery/development journey and decided it was time to share my views of things, and the actions I took to get me to a place where I can write a whole book about it. The fact that I am even typing this out now should be a sign that something I'm doing is working, and it continues to work because I am on a mission to be the best possible version of myself. I think we all should be striving for that. Each and everyone one of us.

I mean, why not?

Let me ask you to do your best to emotionally involve yourself in the principles that follow this message. Let them activate parts of you that haven't been tapped into for quite some time. Let the words stimulate the deepest part of your subconscious and allow them to plant fresh seeds of positivity, growth, truth, inner-badassery, and guidance.

These principles are simple, honest, and...well...blunt. I have used these principles to pull myself out of my own way and to truly be able to start living in a much happier flow of life. I encourage you to really get involved with these principles, I promise they have some power behind them. Apply them to your own life and watch your reality and results shift towards greatness.

I want to say thank you from the truest, most authentic part of my being.

Thank You for allowing me to share.

Always With Love,

Zac

Author's Note

I wanted to include some type of explanation for my title. Although I dip a couple of toes into the water, which you are about to dive into with my preface, I could not help but include this piece to my book. Throughout the past several months a lot has changed in my life. This book was written throughout my time spent in Hawai'i, on the beautiful island of Oahu, and I finished the rest of these pages in my native land of Georgia. Here I sit in my loft, writing by candlelight and enjoying the last remaining vice in my life...caffeine. Fuck, what a journey. I am telling you right now, life is a fucking rollercoaster and you should enjoy every god damn high and low that you can. It's all here to serve you. Make every moment a memory to guide you on this radical pilgrimage. I suppose now is a good time to let you know where this came from. *Radical Pilgrimage*. I first heard this mentioned from my colleague and business partner, Wes Robins.

As I write this, and as you will read later with more detail in this book, I am a Therapeutic Mentor/Coach. I work with youth and young adults ranging from ages 12-25. I am trained and certified as a Cognitive Behavioral Therapist and a Behavior Change Specialist. I specialize in guidance and strategy for young people. I help them to find aim and direction in life. Encouraging them to tap into their innate power that most of us tend to neglect in this life. I sit with them, listen, learn, and do my best to guide them towards their highest self. I believe it is more than easy to become nihilistic in nature and have no purpose when you lack an aim. Something to shoot for. And I practice what I preach, daily. I absolutely fucking love what I do. I am blessed to be able to sit with these young people and share the tools that I have used to heal myself and the ongoing inner work that I engage in on a daily basis, but in the famous words of Ram Dass: "I help people as I work on myself and I work on myself to help people." No one can do your work for you. YOU have to do it. But I can sure as hell can loan you all the tools, knowledge, and experiences I have gathered during my growth and development. And that's what I do daily. Because these youth are on a *Radical Pilgrimage*. Which brings me to the creator of the term, Kathleen S. G. Skott-Myhre. She wrote a beautiful paper titled, "Youth: A Radical Space of Pilgrimage." I pulled some of my favorite passages from this amazing piece to best explain where she is coming from her conceptualization of adolescence:

"Another problem with the reification of the discourse of adolescence as both problematic and transitory is that we cut short the possibilities that lie within this liminal space as we try to rush young people through what could be a highly productive space in order to assuage our own fears."

"We all have various spaces that we retreat to, are drawn to, or run to, as we remake ourselves over and over again. We reflect and consider all of the alternative ways that we can be in the world."

"What happens as we move through this liminal space betweenthat moves, inspires, and transforms? Why do we consider those wonderfullytransformative spaces as something to endure, to "get through" or, in the case ofadolescence, a phase that will pass? What if we began to consider that space in a newway? What if we journeyed alongside those who find themselves in such a space?

18

Whatif we stopped looking at what could be and started paying more attention to what is?"

"I would like to begin to rethink the "phase" of "adolescence" in such a way that itstarts taking on a new language, a new way of being in relationship with young peoplethat offers the possibility of salvaging an important period of time in their (our) lives andoffers us the opportunity to consider the political implications and the opening up ofcreative conversations in new ways with young people. Perhaps a new language willbring to light valuable insight into our own spaces."

"This would mean opening up the possibility of "sitting" with ourselves, the youngpeople, and the adults we encounter in our work in a different sort of way. It wouldsuggest opening up new and creative conversations with them that puts the question ofdesire front and center. As young people in our contemporary society are already engagedin the pilgrimage, we would need to pay particular attention to their phenomenologicalexpertise. We cannot take precisely the same road, because the tasks of liberation aredifferent for each of us. But, the modes of survival in the desert are common to all of us.Engaging seriously with young people, as holding wisdom about the liminal spaces ofindeterminate subjective production, can assist us in understanding our role in thecollective struggle for a common vibrant valorization of living force. We might well learnas parents, law enforcement, social service administrators, psychiatrists, and ourselves aspsychologists that the liminal space of adolescence is full of possibilities, full ofpotentialities. Once we set aside the normative discourse of youth as pathological anddeviant, we can begin to uncover the vast areas of possibility and resource. This hasimplications, not just for youth and our encounters with them, but for us as well. Once welet go of the notion that young people are "unfinished" and need to be

regulated andmanaged, the conversations open up in ways that allow us to let go of our own "lack". Astherapists and as parents, we are being given the opportunity to see ourselves ascompetent and resourceful."

In my recent work with youth I have recognized that it is truly a *Radical Pilgrimage* and Skott-Mhyres view is fucking spot-on. Youth sit in a very unique space through the growth and development of discovering who they are, and I absolutely love the way she describes the journey. When I first set out to write this book, it wasn't geared towards youth. To be completely honest, I did not know what kind of demographic it could/would reach or resonate with. As I moved into doing work with youth and young adults, and as I was finishing this writing, I found myself experiencing divine timing at its finest. The stars aligned, and synchronicity, once again played its part in my life.

As I looked back over these words I realized exactly who I wrote it for, youth. Those going through radical growth and development. This book speaks directly to them, in their own language. I unknowingly, unconsciously wrote this for them. Anything to help guide through the space in which they walk. And I hope with every fiber of my being that it can. Now that doesn't mean that only youth and young adults could apply this information to their life for positive growth , I believe that this book could serve many wherever they're on their path. Principle 12 will explain that. :)

"We cannot always build the future for our youth, but we can build our youth for the future."
-Franklin D. Roosevelt

One More Note....

Ok, ok....I get it. You probably want to start reading this already. One more thing. I am a huge fan of repetition. I think to fully grasp the meaning and have the ability to apply it to your life, then you must be involved deeply in the information being given and have a true understanding. Over and over and over. At that end of each Principle I have included a chance for you to perform written exercises:

- Key Points To Remember (for YOU)

- Challenge Exercise

Reviewing the highlights of the Principle and then performing a thought provoking, fresh perspective giving, deep, and critical thinking exercise, only helps to create more energy and a deeper resonance with the meaning of each piece of knowledge shared. Truly understanding through the process of repetition will assist in the action piece of it.

You see, the more we understand something, the more confidence we build into that "thing." The more confidence we build, the easier it will be to apply the necessary courage needed to move you into action towards the chosen desire, goal, or whatever it is you're going after. Each one building from the previous will create the momentum also required to cultivate the persistence that will be guaranteed you need along your journey.

"Knowledge is Power. Knowledge without application is USELESS."
- Bruce Lee

Principle

A fundamental truth or proposition that serves as the foundation for a system of belief or behavior or for a chain of reasoning.

PRINCIPLE 1

"Get Some Brutal Truth"

I first heard the term "Brutal Truth" from my boss, Andrew B., when I was Department Head of Sales with a well-known health club in my hometown of Atlanta, GA. This guy was a great leader because he was honest, direct, compassionate, and fair. All the qualities that you would want in a leader. And when I heard him use this, it stuck with me. Now, even though it stuck with me, I never really applied it in my own life. Why would I? Remember? I used to suck. Nowadays, I consistently use brutal truth. I apply that shit everywhere. It's the only way to move past your own bullshit. It's the only way to get to where you want to be. And it's the only way to be able to move forward with authenticity, which in my opinion goes hand in hand with integrity. And trust me, both are needed on the path you are about to embark on. Learn to create the ability to gain some of it in your life. Truth, that is.

I had too. Like I said, I wasn't too keen on using any type of brutal truth in my life. I was good at hiding from it--Running from it even. I thought maybe if I ignore the things in my life that are falling apart, then maybe they will just go away. I was lying to myself, and rationalizing to myself why things are the way they were.

Rationalizing- *The art of Ration(ing) LIES to yourself.*

Can you relate? Is there anything currently in your life that you know you should change, but just keep pushing it down, ignoring it? Lying to yourself, hoping and maybe even wishing that it will just disappear? Well I hate to tell you (not really) but it doesn't and will never work like that.

I decided after my second divorce, bankruptcy, DUI, substance abuse, sex addiction, steroid abuse, two repossessed vehicles, no money in the bank, low self-esteem, anger issues, and simply zero direction in life that I needed to make a change. And it always seems to work out like this for most of us. We require some type of catastrophe, or some type of life-changing event, or when our back is completely against the wall to decide to go in another direction. Although the signs have been there the whole time, we continue to play out the roles we have accepted to play.

Why is that? Fear. We are scared. It's as simple as that. We fear change, we fear getting honest with ourselves. It's like, "Me? I am the cause of all my problems? No, I couldn't be!" We are scared to get honest with ourselves. And THAT is the truth. Most of us don't realize that we are stuck in a cycle of playing out the same type of days over and over. Involving ourselves in the same behaviors, actions, and decisions that lead us to wherever we are going. And all the while expecting something different to happen. That is called insanity, my friends. And I was an *insane* man. Now all those things mentioned earlier, they didn't happen all at once, and that's almost the sad thing about it. It was gradual. I allowed it to sneak up on me, I allowed the years to go by and continued to proudly play my role as the victim. I thought I was a victim. A victim of life, and how it was just beating me down. I had the mindset that I was just a pawn in this whole game. Just being moved around without any type of control. A lot of us play the victim role, and I should've received an Emmy or even the famed Oscar for my performance. Yeah, facts. Year after year I continued to lie to myself about things changing for me, and yet getting the same results. Different forms, but ultimately same results. Players were changing, but the game remained the exact same. But what was I doing to change them? Not a damn thing! Nothing. Nada. Zilch.

So why do we continue to believe that something magical might come along and completely change our lives? Because we are ignorant to the fact that we first need to step back and get some brutal truth in our lives. We need to be able to be completely honest with ourselves and say "hey, I am fucking up." My second divorce was the ultimate catalyst for my transition from victim to warrior. I had nothing left in me. I couldn't even muster up any kind of fight to keep my role alive and kicking. I let it go. I got honest and told myself that I could no longer live like this. I just couldn't do it anymore. And if I did, where would I be in five, ten, even fifteen years? And the thought of that whipped me in to shape. Quick.

The feeling inside of me was so bad that I didn't care what I had to do to experience a different life, I *HAD* to do it. I knew I was in for a shitstorm of change, but I knew coming out the other end and going through whatever it was I had to in order to be in a different position, I was all in, baby!

So, if you haven't realized it by now... YOU and only YOU are responsible for every type of result you have in your life at this current moment. It's ok though, you are here, you want to expand, you want to learn, maybe find some strategies, methods, principles, perspectives to live your life in a better way. To live your life with more grace and ease, with less confusion, chaos, and cyclical habits that have you stuck on the treadmill of life; moving all the time, but not going *anywhere*.

Take a step back, and look at your life. No, I mean really take a HUGE step back and gain a very good insight and overview of where you currently are. Based on our thoughts, decisions, actions, and beliefs in life we receive feedback. This feedback is another way of saying "Results."

What are your current results? What is your feedback saying to you?

I encourage you to cultivate the ability to get brutally honest with yourself. Step #1 of How To Not Suck...yeah, let's start there. This is the only way to start stepping in the direction into your true alignment. This is also the only way you're going to know if the feedback you have been receiving is "negative" or "positive," and whether you are heading in the "right" direction or walking down the path of self-sabotage. Most of us are scared to get honest with ourselves in any capacity.

What are you afraid of? To know that YOU are fucking up? Yeah, I can understand that. I know I was scared out of my mind to get honest with myself, but I had to. I could no longer live with the results I was getting. I *had* to go in another direction. I had to try something different, but there came a point where I told myself I would rather feel the intense pain of honesty then to keep heading down a path that was pushing me further away from my true self and to be able to live a joy filled life.

But think about this, my friends...

What's scarier? The notion of getting brutally honest with yourself and your current results? Or continuing to lie to yourself and living out your days in complete misalignment, frustration, and often leading to resentment, and missing out on a life filled with more abundance (in every department) than you could ever imagine?

Choose. Choose wisely.

It's *completely* ok to say, "Hey, I am not happy with me!" It's ok to say, "My current results suck and how do I fix it?" Understand that when you have this thought that this is a breakthrough in and of itself. The fact that you can recognize something like this is major! So, congratulations to you if you can resonate with this notion and look in the mirror and say, "I suck."

Ok. Let's give it a shot.

I challenge you right now to stop reading, go to a mirror, look yourself in the eyes and say:

I suck and I am ready to change. I am ready to gain a clear insight of where I am currently at, and what needs to be done in order to regain my true power and step into alignment with who I am meant to be, I am done playing the victim and I am ready to be a fucking warrior!

Was that weird? Did it make you uncomfortable? Was it a challenge to step into the unknown and perform an exercise like this one? Good. Being uncomfortable is the first step into growth. It forces you to grow. It commands you to grow. You have no other choice but to grow. To progress! It levels you up!

Start getting very comfortable with being uncomfortable if you want to continue this journey into self-discovery/ empowerment/growth. It is in these moments where we can truly thrive. Realize that right now, reading this, you have started the momentum of change within yourself. Bravo!

I continually look at myself in the mirror and look into my eyes and have a heart-to-heart with me. Yeah, maybe it is weird, but if anyone is going to do it, it might as well be.... me. I know me best. And *you* know *you* best. Now you might have gotten estranged from the real you, but he/she is in there. Maybe waiting on permission to step out and own shit. Waiting on the chance to say "Fucking finally! YES! Let's do this baby!"

Get out of your own way. Gain an understanding that YOU are possibly holding YOU back by not being able to be honest.

In order to gain a true and clear understanding of your current situation in life, you must first take a **personal inventory**. This is 100% the first step towards getting brutally honest with yourself. Take an inventory of your life. From my consistent studying, self-educating, and life application, I have learned and adopted that there are four life departments in which you can take a detailed inventory. And they are:

• Spiritual- Soul

• Emotional- Heart

• Mental- Mind

• Physical-Health

Have you ever thought of it this way? We have all heard the word balance as it pertains to your life. So have you ever thought of what you are actually balancing? Most of the time you hear work-life balance...blah, blah, blah. Ok, so you're telling me that these two things are the only thing we balance? So what's life? Yeah, what is life? I will tell you that in my humble opinion it is these four departments. They hardly have anything to do with our external world and more than ever to do with our internal world. And we all should be working towards balancing all these departments. Well, wait a second, not just balancing these, but thriving in each of these categories.

What do these 4 departments currently look like in your life?

Let me ask you:

What are you doing right now to consistently grow in these four departments?

Something? Anything? I will wait...

Ok, time is up. Look, if you are like I used to be, these "departments" of life never crossed my mind. The way I used to be was: well if I have a rocking body and money, I am good to go. I will have everything I need...right? Jesus...can you imagine? Maybe you can. Maybe you can relate to this mindset. I was waaaaaaay off from my true nature. Gee, and I wonder why I was consistently getting shit results in my life. I had never once sat down with myself and pointed out what I could be doing better and actively pursuing growth in these four departments. I urge you to act on each of these departments and seek where you could improve, where you're doing well, and create an action plan to assist with the nurturing and growth of each of these.

See Principle 9: Set Some Damn Goals.

Get out a sheet of paper and list the four departments of your life and rate each one. With the utmost honesty you can muster, ask yourself what you are ACTIVELY doing to seek growth within these? This is such an amazing exercise and NEEDED to even start in the direction of working on yourself in order to live at your full potential. How can you possibly find a starting point or what direction to go in when you don't really have an idea where you are at? You must first take an inventory on yourself. Do some research on you, take a bird's eye view approach and really take a deep dive into all of it. Set some time aside and go to a quiet area where you can concentrate. Get serious about it. You don't have to be grim, but take a serious approach. I promise you it can really change your life.

But first...

You need to know something about you. You need to be able to know exactly who you are dealing with. Do you know yourself? Truly? Do you understand where your beliefs come from? Do you know the program that you operate from? The paradigm in which controls the very direction of your results? Let this next principle explain a little more so you can have a better vision of just who you actually are.

"A truth is what it is. A lie; a thought out deception more brutal than a truth could ever be."
-Charlotte Armstrong

Key Points To Remember

Brutal Truth Challenge

Please List 3 Brutal Truths you can confront yourself with.

_____

_____

_____

*What actions will you take to start thriving in the
4 Internal Life Departments?*

Spiritual-

_____

_____

_____

Mental-

_____

_____

_____

Emotional-

_____

_____

_____

Physical-

_____

_____

_____

PRINCIPLE 2

"Know Who You're Identifying With"

The consciousness of your own identity.

What is *your* identity? Who have you been identifying with? It's an extremely important question to ask yourself when you want to head down the road of personal development and empowerment. You must be able to separate yourself (in a sense) from the ego. You must understand what the ego represents. It is simply an illusion. It's who you *think* you are, and for a good portion of our time here it is what most of us have identified with. It's a dangerous game to **solely** identify with your ego. I truly believe it never goes away. It's always going to be in there; however, consider the duality of who we are and what we are. We are both. Good and Evil. Masculine and Feminine. Yin and Yang...it goes on. Learn to know what is feeding your ego and what is feeding your soul. You cannot stand in both. Once you can step back and get honest with yourself (see Principle 1) then you are headed down a beautiful path. If you can move forward with the notion that you have been the one fucking up, this becomes a dramatic first step into stripping away the ego--well maybe not all of it, but some.

Let me explain.

A good friend of mine, Wes Robins, shared a book with me titled: *Toward a Psychology of Awakening- Buddhism, Psychotherapy, and the Path of Personal and Spiritual*

Transformation by John Welwood, and in this book, he speaks about "Ego Strength and Egolessness," and how Eastern Psychology and Western Psychology view the Ego and how it pertains to our mental well-being. Both stand on opposite sides on how we should define the ego and what it fully represents. Welwood believes that there can be common ground found between the two perspectives of it. While Eastern Psychology looks beyond the notion of a strong ego toward a larger quality of being that is egoless, or free of the constraints of the boundless self-sense.

While Western psychotherapy emphasizes the need for a strong ego, defined in terms of impulse control, self-esteem, and competence in worldly functioning. He asks what would it mean if these two philosophies and views on how the ego pertains to human life could forge some common ground of understanding? I believe that it could be. That's why I mentioned above about it not all stripping away. Again, I believe that it's always going to be in there. I believe that denying that would only be creating some type of resistance in your energy. Fully accepting the self is accepting *all* parts of yourself, not just what you consider "good" parts. Remember the duality part earlier? Yeah, that. We are both. So I believe in not fully stripping away this part of you. Use it. It can be utilized in some sort of positive fashion.

OK, So back to that question…What have you been identifying with? Who? Who is it that you think you are? What have you been led to believe? Ah, yes…believe…or should I say belief! What have you been conditioned into thinking about yourself? What story have you told yourself? What personal beliefs do you encompass? Are they severely limiting your ability to perform well in the departments of life? If you are reading these words at this moment, I highly encourage you to STOP and take out a notebook and start writing out on some of these questions. Get granular with it too. Do not rush through this process. We must really start to identify what type of belief systems we have been operating from for most of our life.

WE MUST!

From ages 0-7 we do not possess the consciousness that we develop over the years, and the prefrontal cortex is not even close to being fully developed. That's the part of the brain that is in "charge" of planning complex cognitive behavior, personality expression, decision making, and moderating social behavior. Within those first seven years all we are doing is simply recording behavior and absorbing all that is around us. We are like big sponges. It is between these ages when we are the most impressionable. Yet at this age we lack the ability to filter through the bullshit (and that's what most of it is) and come up with our own path. So what do we do? We follow the leader. Unfortunately, with most, it doesn't stop there in the early childhood years. Most of us carry this same belief system and operate from it for life, but kudos to you for stepping the fuck up, grabbing this book and figuring your shit out.

Yes, ok, back to it. We follow what our parents, close relatives, teachers, etc. are doing and saying and believing...yikes! Now let me state for the record, your family members are not *bad* people--no, but maybe our parents and relatives absorbed and adopted certain paradigms of beliefs that weren't so self-serving. That's all I'm saying. Also, I carry the belief that you cannot give someone something that you do not possess yourself. So, whatever they were handed and applied in their life, you can bet your ass you took in some of that too.

But that's ok. I am telling you right now that the first step to deconstructing some belief systems is to identify them and say, "Do I even agree with this anymore?" "What do I really believe about myself?" There is that word again. What do you *believe* about yourself? We tell stories about ourselves every day. EVERY

DAY! So, what are you continually saying? A brief reminder-- the subconscious (you know that thing that controls 95% of your action/behaviors/decisions?) it works mainly on what is constantly repeated.

I ask you, again, what stories do you tell about yourself all day long? Is it the ego you consistently identify with? Are you acting in your own true nature from your own belief systems? Really think about this. I once had a roommate and every single morning he would wake up, come out to the kitchen and state, "I'm exhausted." I am not too sure how long he had been saying that, but the short four months I lived with him, he said that every. single. day. Now at that time, I wasn't at the consciousness level I possess now in order to understand why this guy was usually not in the best mood, but can you imagine if he continued to say that every single day? What do you think is happening? By repeating this affirmation over and over and over, he is slowly emotionally getting attached to the notion that he is exhausted all the time. If you say a lie long enough, you will start to believe it. This is just the way it works. What lies have you been operating from?

Have you ever thought about it?

What stories do you tell about yourself all day long? Small things that we might not notice. What agreements are you making without even knowing it? We must proceed with caution when you speak about yourself, and we must proceed with even more caution as to not get emotionally attached if it is self-sabotaging. It works the same way with belief systems--whatever we have told ourselves about ourselves for an extended period we begin to believe, internalize, and it then externalizes and shows up in our physical realities. We will go into this a bit more in Principle 4.

Now think about this.

It's not only what you have been saying about yourself, but also the opinions from others that you have agreed with and identified with.

Understand this now before we move ahead--just because someone states an opinion about you, it does not have to be your reality, it does not make it true, and it does not make it real. The only way it can manifest in your own life is when you emotionally attach yourself to that notion and continuously act out on it. You don't have to agree with it. There is way more on this topic a little later, don't you worry. But again, in your younger years you may not have possessed a strong mindset and you agreed with people's opinions of you or what you should be doing with yourself and your path. That's why this exercise is so vitally important for your inner growth. You must identify the things that do not truly represent who and what you are.

Identify those things that you know in your heart you cannot identify with anymore. This is what I believe represents the ego, the "identity." What we have unconsciously consumed during the duration of this life experience and held within ourselves becomes our identity. And we do the best we can to uphold the image or the ego. It was my false self-image that allowed me to play the victim for so long, and turned my life into utter chaos, which ultimately led me down a path of self-defeating actions.

Know this now:

We operate strictly from our belief system/paradigm/program, whatever you want to call it. Our actions and behaviors are aligned and in total synchronicity with the program we are operating from. So, in order to make our beliefs true for ourselves, we have formed habits and behaviors to support that particular program. So, your program (or better put, mass of habits) is what controls the daily actions you take, and the daily thoughts you agree with. That's why it is necessary to start questioning what it is you are operating from and from what source. This is vital when you want to head down the road of personal development/empowerment/discovery.

Let me ask you this: Who's got you talked into doing whatever it is you're doing? Is it the higher side of your personality? Your soul, your intuition? Or is it this "image" or "identity" that has been built over the years by someone else's beliefs, thoughts, and opinions? Question this. Many times. All the time.

Let's do this just once more.

I really want to drive this home.

Who and what do you identify with? What self-image do you have of yourself? Is it yours that you consistently defend and try your best to agree with? Is this identity truly serving your highest self? Is it leading you down a path of higher consciousness? Is it creating and designing a life that you are fulfilled by? Is your program serving you in the best possible way?

OR

Have you been identifying with a possible false self-image? Is this your own identity? Is this coming from years of absorption and unconsciously made agreements? Who is representing your decisions? Actions? Thought? Beliefs?

Are you consciously aware enough that you and only you are deciding what kind of program to operate from?

We must be able to cipher through this type of conditioning to find out *who* and *what* we truly are, and how we want to continue to live. I am not saying live your life in solitude until you can really get a clear vision. Although solitude will help drown out the noise of the world, I don't recommend you become a recluse, but surrounding yourself with the right type of people will have such a profound effect on you when you go down this road. Having the right kind of people who are supporting the newly emerging you can create the ability for you to stay on this chosen path a little easier. Which leads us to our next principle.

"The value of identity of course is that so often it comes with purpose."
- Richard Grant

Key Points To Remember

Know Who You're Identifying With Challenge

Please list 1 or more belief systems that you have been identifying with that may not be true for you now.

_____

_____

_____

What new belief system(s) will you create and emotionally involve yourself in to replace the old?

_____

_____

_____

PRINCIPLE 3

"Check Your Circle"

Who are your "friends"?

I put that word in quotations only because I believe it to be an extremely misused word. It gets thrown around way too often, and we find ourselves surrounded by all these "friends" that really do not care about our wellbeing at all.

You see, you must tread lightly on who you call a friend these days. Look at your closest friend circle. The five people who are closest to you. The people you involve yourself with on a daily/ weekly basis. Now really start to think about the types of people they are.

Wait.

Before we go any further, I must disclose that I am not encouraging you to judge your friends, or anyone for that matter. This exercise is only for stating the facts of your circle, and to discover if the people you surround yourself with are good for *YOUR* path.

At one time in my life I realized who my "friends" were. When I was about thirty years old I decided to dive into the world of competitive bodybuilding.

Wait.

Let's rewind.

Before that, my *then* group of friends partied...hard. Oh... did we ever. We did cocaine, loads of alcohol, weed, MDMA, and honestly whatever was accessible to us. That's who I involved myself with. That's the path I was on, which went on for some time. I was unconsciously and consciously (in some way) *choosing* to partake in shit that was driving me into a darker side of life. I mean this was turning out to be an almost a daily ritual.

But, like most of us, we think it's ok because EVERYONE around us is doing it, too. So naturally, I was like, ok...so I guess I do this now. I didn't even think twice about how these activities were debilitating me on each and every level. Now, as much as we partied, we all also worked out. It is important to mention that this is when my steroid abuse became a huge part of my life. In the midst of all this, I decided that I wanted to be involved in competitive bodybuilding, which only left me with one choice--I had to choose to stop partying, stop drinking, stop drugging, stop with the sleepless nights, stop with the bullshit activities that I so willingly allowed myself to be apart of. So, naturally I slowly removed myself from that crowd. At first, they laughed, judged, criticized, and they asked, "What's wrong with you dude?"

It wasn't easy to make this choice. I mean, these were my *"boys,"* right? These were my "friends". No, not even close. Do you think that one of these guys came to my shows? Supported my change in lifestyle? Encouraged me? Uplifted me? Called to see how the prep was coming for my first show? NO. Negative. Not even close. I realized then that these were not my friends at all. They were just a group of dudes that were all involved with the same self-defeating behaviors, and it was easy to stay in that type of vibration and situation because EVERYONE was doing it. I believe that most of us are caught up in the same mindset. We don't even question what we are doing because our group of "friends" are all doing it too. We do not even question if the daily activities we involve ourselves in with these people are leading us down a road of misery or bliss. The last thing that we want is to be shunned by the people that we supposedly care about and to ask who actually cares about us, right? That's tough to even face. Hey man, I get it. I was there. Luckily, I so badly wanted to compete in bodybuilding, that it pulled me away from that type of lifestyle. It pulled me away from the self-sabotaging behaviors that would've led me down a road of more self-destruction.

I see this all the time. I hear people complain about how they feel, the lack of money in their account, the constant gossiping, backstabbing, and the let-downs that they experience with the people they hang out with. Yet, so few of us are willing to realize that these people do not give a FUCK about you or your well-being, and if you continue to go down this road, without ever questioning who you let into your life, then you are in no position to complain about it.

There it is, some **brutal truth** for you. I am not scared. I am not scared to share and express to you my story or the fact that if you can resonate with any of this information then you should take a long hard look at your circle.

Back to it, though, ok, so what types of behaviors do they involve themselves in? What are their hobbies? What type of words, slang, verbiage do they allow to come from their lips? What type of music do they listen to? What are their views on the world? How is their mental outlook? What are their habits? Do they have ambitions, dreams, goals? Do they strive to do better? To be better? How do they treat other people outside your circle? When you hang around your "friends" do they encourage you? Do they push you to be your best possible self? When you get together is it an uplifting experience, or is it one that leaves you feeling drained? Is the talk you have filled with gossip? Or is it filled with kind words of people?

Ok, I think we have covered enough to stimulate your mind with questions you ought to be asking yourself about the types of people you allow into your life. If most of your answers were on the not so positive side, I highly encourage you to take a step back from this circle and question if it is doing YOU any good.

You see, you will become the people you spend the most time with. Period. You will adopt their habits, behaviors, verbiage, their mental outlook, their perspectives. You must be cautious with these types of things in life. This is a serious matter, not grim. Well, it could be, depending on the caliber of friends you allow into your circle. You must consistently check who you invite into your life. I am not saying people are bad, but people might have some types of behaviors that are not good for YOU and YOUR path.

That's a fact. But it goes back to the first step in this whole process. Get real fucking honest with yourself. Especially on this part. People will stay in relationships when they are miserable just because they do not want to hurt the other person. I can completely empathize and understand that notion, but what about YOU? You are willing to hurt YOU but not someone else? YOU must live with YOUR decisions daily, and it is completely ok to separate yourself from people who are draining your energies and shifting your focus away from things that could benefit you.

Get honest. Make a list if you must. This is a form of self-love and self-respect. This is setting boundaries at an all-time high. Take inventory. This is what this is. I never said it wouldn't be challenging, because shifting your mindset to benefit the rest of your life is not an easy process, but it is doable. I promise you. But as nasty as this sounds, I believe it must be done. With honesty, integrity, and love. I am not stating that these are bad people, or to even cut ties with them completely, but if you go through the series of questions above and the answers you find within are not stellar, then I ask you to not involve yourself with them as much.

Take a step back. See what is different when you start spending time with yourself and people who can uplift you, and you can do the same for them. I would even go as far to explain that you want to experience a positive change with some things in your life and that you will not be around as much and will be seeking the best for you. If your "friends" do not encourage you to do what is best for you, then I wouldn't waste another minute explaining myself (which you don't have to do anyways, I am just throwing the idea out there).

I encourage you to seek out people that are doing the things that you want to do. Seek out the people that are goal-oriented, have higher standards set for themselves, and who seek out greatness in others. Surrounding yourself with these types of people will only enhance your life, in every aspect. It seems weird to even say this, but hang out with people who are better than you.

I know that sounds a bit harsh, but I think it stings just enough to get your attention. Sometimes that's what we need to get a little blood pumping. Get us a little pissed off. Get serious about personal development. Get serious about YOU. This is YOUR life and YOUR mental wellbeing at stake here. So yeah, hang out with people who are better than you, and what I really mean by that is that hanging around people who might have adopted healthier, self-benefiting/serving habits earlier in life that can show you how to be better. To do better. To earn more, to give more, to have a better character, to be better in the marketplace.

Hang around success man! That's it. Why would you want to involve yourself with people who have zero ambition and who are completely content with living in mediocrity? Living in quiet desperation? No thank you. Wise up and start taking that personal inventory we spoke about earlier. Do it. Now. Start moving in the direction of greatness.

Look, for example, if you wanted to get better at a sport and you only played with people that were just as good as you or maybe slightly less talented, what level would you stay at? How much better could you really become? How much could you learn? Grow? Excel? Master? What direction would you be headed in? Now, if you surround yourself with people who are excelling in areas you would like, or have certain achievements on their resume, or they are operating at a level in life in which you desire, then the view will start looking a little different.

In other words, *surround yourself with success*. Success leaves clues, they have blueprints in place for what they have already achieved, and possess the "know-how" to get to that level. I am not saying completely remove people from your life, but if it isn't a good energy exchange and everyone that is involved in that circle isn't growing and becoming better, then maybe you can limit your time with them.

Spend less time with people who are not the best for your path and where you are headed and more time with the people who can lift your spirits, encourage you, push you (if needed). I cannot stress this to you enough, having the right kind of people around you is so vital to your success. It is vital to your growth both interior and exterior. Surround yourself with kind, good-hearted people. Pay attention to how your "friends" treat others. Watch how they treat people who are not close to them. It might seem a bit off, but if your friends are doing more putting down than inspiring and uplifting things to people....back off.

I repeat, this is not an easy task, but if you want to get serious about How To Not Suck, this must be done. If you really attached yourself to Principle #1 then continue down that road of discovery.

I also highly encourage you to get yourself really involved in this next principle. We ALL can use this friendly reminder.

"Not all toxic people are cruel and uncaring. Some love us dearly. Many of them have good intentions. Most are toxic to our being, simply because...they aren't inherently bad people, but they aren't the right people for us. And as hard as it is, we have to let them go."
-Danielle Koepke

Key Points To Remember

Check Your Circle Challenge

Please list 3 or more self-defeating behavior(s) you involve yourself in with your immediate circle.

_____

_____

_____

Now that you have identified it (them), what action will you take to change it (them)?

_____

_____

_____

Principle 4

"Watch Your Mouth, and Maybe.... Shut it"

You must proceed with caution when it comes to the words you use to describe things. Words are powerful. Words are vibration, words are energy, words.....well they matter.

This Principle goes hand in hand with Principle 2.

Words can shape our reality so fast that we won't know what hit us. What we continually say about ourselves, other people, places, or things will have some type of effect on our external reality. Especially when we become emotionally attached to them, or consistently repeat them. Remember, your subconscious mind (ya know, the thing that controls 95% of our behavior?) works off repetition. Habits are formed from repetition. How do you think things become automatic? By repetition. You repeat something so much it becomes second nature. Yes, even your reality. So I ask you now, what do you say all day? Remember in Principle 2 how we talked about the stories we tell all day long. So, what kind of storyteller are you? What things do you consistently say about the things in your life? The relationships, the experiences, the money, the activities, and most importantly, you? Everything we use to describe these things will ultimately shape it, but have we ever stopped and thought about the shape of things for us? What type of reality are we molding for ourselves with our *word-clay*? Are you crafting a beautiful work of art, something by the likes of a *Michelangelo*? Or are you drafting up something that looks like a four-year-old colored it with the use of only two crayons? Dull ones too. Seriously, what kind of reality are you constructing with your words? The way in which we describe things, perceive things, and place meanings on things in our life all use the gift of language to define. Language is beautiful, but only if beautifully used. Some say that language was created to hide emotion, and while I somewhat agree with that, I cannot help but think that pairing these two can really create something amazing for yourself. We can benefit from emotionally attaching ourselves to how we describe and define things. By using a positive vibration, one of love, faith, and passion, it will manifest some of the most gorgeous opportunities and blessings you could ever experience in this life. Now, if you get emotionally involved and translate that energy in a negative fashion, an experience of anger, fear, and toxicity will surmount no doubt.

Sit and think about how you use language daily to place meaning on this life experience. How do you describe your days? Really stop and think about this. How do YOU define your days and all that is in them? Is this used in a repetitive manner? Remember that roommate I had? You know the one that said he was exhausted every day, guess what? He was fucking exhausted everyday...he even looked exhausted. That thought that he held inside his creative and subconscious mind and became emotionally attached to created the reality of him being tired all the time! By fixating this thought within himself, it caused a certain vibration through his body in which we call emotion or feeling, which caused the behavior and actions to keep him exhausted. You see when we have an idea firmly planted into our subconscious mind, and it becomes rooted, and you continue to water and feed that seed of an idea, then it will cause your body to move into a certain vibration and that's what causes the actions and behaviors (habits) to support the idea (program/paradigm) that you're subconscious mind is operating from.

Got it?

Did I lose you?

Ok...

Do you have an understanding of how your subconscious mind works off of *autosuggestion?* Autosuggestion defined as the hypnotic or subconscious adoption of an idea that one has originated oneself, e.g. through repetition of verbal statements to oneself in order to change behavior. I first heard about autosuggestion through Napoleon Hill. If you are not familiar with this man then I recommend that you get really familiar with his philosophies and his principles, and if I'm being completely honest, he has inspired me on this path of self-discovery and development more than I can really attest to. Hell, even this book, and I'm sure hundreds of others, have been inspired by his teachings and philosophies. His book *Think and Grow Rich* has a large part written on the use of autosuggestion. I highly recommend reading Hill's book.

No matter what "data" you're feeding your subconscious, it will give you the "answer" in the form of your results and your experience. Negative or positive your subconscious mind *does not care.* It is simply taking "orders" from your thoughts, beliefs, *words*, feelings, and taking that information and creating your reality for you. So what kind of "data" is in there? What beliefs, thoughts, feelings, and words do you give it to externalize into your current reality. What is in there currently? What will you start feeding it knowing this?

I state this again: The subconscious mind controls 95% of our behaviors, decisions, and actions, and if we are not conscious of this or have a complete understanding of this, then it can lead to quite the challenging life. Especially if you are trying to get results and you do not have a clear understanding of how it truly functions. By consistently repeating certain words, phrases, and placing distinctive definitions on things over, and over, and over, and over again it will soon have the complete reaction to the action that you're performing. The reaction being...that's right, you guessed it, your results!

What type of autosuggestion are you using daily? How is your vocabulary? What are you feeding your mind with the meanings place on things? What type of thoughts and words are you attached to in relation to your life?

Let me ask you this: I would like for you to take a moment and think of the things you have relationships with in your life. Like your job, marriage, finances, health, etc., and out of these areas mentioned, which one isn't maybe where you would like it to be? Which one (maybe not even mentioned) is suffering in some way. Could one use some help? Or maybe a little bit more nurturing? After thinking about it, I would like for you to think about how you describe this certain thing. How do you talk about it? Do you talk about it often? What idea (program/paradigm) is it operating from? What have you become emotionally attached to in defining it the way you currently do?

Take a minute. Write it out if you need to.

Did you get some clear vision of how you talk and feel about this certain thing? Were you able to use some *brutal truth*? Have you come to terms with the way you're describing it, and maybe even daily, is causing you to feel a certain way about it? Maybe even shaping the reality that revolves around the chosen area?

Could you think of any other words or meanings you could place on it to define it in some positive type of way? Change the *suggestions* that you have *automatically* been attaching? Change the vibration in which your words (and emotions that fuel it) hold?

In doing that, do you think it could take some other form for you? Do you think if you started to use words and feelings that are tuned in to a more positive frequency and vibration that it will actually cause you and your body (instrument of creation) to move into a different course of behavior (habit) and action? Would this area improve? YES! Of course it will. It will completely *transform* your relationship and the reality (results) that it produces. In his book, *Awaken The Giant Within,* Tony Robbins has an entire chapter on Transformational Vocabulary. It's amazing, and the first time I read it, it hit me hard. So many of the simple things that we describe in our daily habits, we describe in such a shit way, and we don't even notice it!

The challenge from earlier is a big one, I know. But an important one. So, maybe let's move our focus and start building the muscle for this with the little things we define in our lives. Here is a list of words that we use every day, to put meanings on ourselves (mostly) that we often do not think matter too much, and a list of words we can use to replace them.

"Be sure to taste your words before you spit them out."
-Unknown

All the following examples are about YOU. These examples were borrowed from the monster of a book: *Awaken the Giant Within,* by the master Tony Robbins. Because honestly, he is the man, and I LOVE his examples and needed to share them. I firmly believe this is a great place to start. And I also believe that if we can shift how we describe ourselves, and ourselves in certain challenges, then we can use that momentum to start a shift in how we describe other things in our life.

I am...

Frustrated --> Challenged

Confused --> Curious

Nervous --> Excited

Furious --> Passionate

Exhausted --> Recharging

Jealous --> Overloving

Stupid --> Learning

Terrible --> Different

Sick --> Cleansing

Hurt --> Surprised

Insulted --> Misinterpreted

Lonely --> Available

Irritated --> Stimulated

Angry --> Disenchanted

Afraid --> Uncomfortable

Depressed -->Not on top of it

Embarrassed --> Aware

Impatient --> Anticipating

Lazy --> Storing Energy

Lost --> Searching

I hope this list helps get you started on transforming your words. It's a great start, and I know that can help shape your relationship with the things that matter most in our life. Starting with YOU.

After you can step back and fully analyze the words and emotions attached to the words you describe yourself with daily, go even further than that. Go deeper. Deeper than you have before.

Find something that you have a challenging time formulating a healthy relationship with.

For me, it was money. Big surprise there! I had such a shit relationship with money in my life because of how I talked about it and emotionally felt about it.

Hence the repos, bankruptcy, etc. I had to question if the way in which I was emotionally describing this thing, this ENERGY, was affecting the reality of it in my life. And the answer was, yes, of course. So, I changed the way I talked about it. I planted a different seed in my mind about my relationship with money. I became attached to a different meaning with money.. I used the practice of autosuggestion to change my relationship and the effect that it had with my current reality of it. I was then moved into a different vibration, and in return it caused my body (instrument of creation) to act and behave differently, which caused my reality to change. I highly encourage you to do the same. Start with you and then let that energy grow into the other areas that could very well be suffering and suppressed from the way you speak about them.

Speaking about suffering and suppression, if you start applying this next principle in your life, those words will not even have a place to reside in your life. Applying this principle will liberate you in ways you could never imagine. The level of freedom that can be achieved through this is *limitless*.

"Creative Words: Generate Energy."

"Negative Words: Drain Energy."
-Robert Schuler

Key Points To Remember

Watch Your Mouth Challenge

Please list 3 phrases you consistently use to describe an area of your life or yourself that could be self-defeating.

_____

_____

_____

What type of Transformational Vocabulary could you use in their place that would be more supportive of your well-being?

_____

_____

_____

Principle 5

"Stop Giving a Fuck"

One thing that has been a recurring theme in my life around the time that I have decided to write this book, is the fact that so many (and I mean SOOOOOOOOOOO many) people give such a huge fuck about how people judge and view them. As a collective, we are beyond terrified about what people will think of us. That's why I carry around the notion that culture is not your friend. Conforming is not going to do you any good. Hence the term "Keeping up with Joneses" is fucking garbage. And by the way, who the hell are these people that I should be keeping up with? They are ahead of me? In what? Life? Bahahahahahaha. Yeah, ok dude.

And that's why I have a complete understanding as to why when I decided to step out and do my own thing, I knew that I would be viewed as different, or an outlaw of some sort, or hell maybe even crazy. But I refuse to let opinions, which, by the way, is the absolute cheapest fucking commodity on earth, run my life. Who am I to give a shit whether someone approves of the way I'm living my chosen path? Why? Really ask yourself why you should even give two righteous fucks as to why someone has something to say about you? Or some type of "answer" as to how you should be doing life?

We involve ourselves so much in others opinions that it gets us far away from our true selves. It leads us down a path of resentment, misalignment, depression, and a constant state of unhappiness. It truly does. How is it going to do you any good by living by someone else's standards? What the fuck do they know? (Do we have an F-word counter yet?) Seriously though, do you ever stop and think how crazy this really is? I hear this ALL the time. People are so scared of what people will say. So, in reality, have you ever stopped and asked what is truly going to happen when and IF they do say something or judge you in some way? What is going to happen? Are you going to be arrested and taken to some weird court of your friends where they all sit on the jury and the verdict comes out that this is, in fact, the stupidest thing you could ever imagine?

I mean really, dude; what is going to happen if you stop caring what others think and say about your life, your journey? For one, it is extremely liberating. It allows you to fall into your own flow of life, your own chosen path. I have such a deep belief that that's where most of the unhappiness comes from in our life. That AND the fact that life isn't happening like it's supposed to, and that we are not even aware of the life we are living is, in most cases, not something that we have consciously chosen. We continually play out the roles of others and adopt them as our own. Why? We are supposed to be fucking unicorns, man. I say this because we are all one, yes, I agree with that notion, but we must try to understand that although we operate from one source of energy, we are all unique expressions of that energy. And that's what makes the world so dope. The diversity. What we all uniquely bring to the table of life. Our special talents and gifts that the creator has blessed us with. They are ours and we have been given each a different gift (in my opinion) to share with the world to help raise the collective consciousness into a vibration of love and growth. So, how can we do that if we are constructing our lives with the materials that others hand us and not our own? How is that doing you any good?

Pssst. Let me tell you a secret...

75

IT ISN'T DOING ANY GOOD!

Again, that's where I believe a lot of our unhappiness stems from. Sure, it's cool at first. Hey! Look at me everybody! I am doing what *EVERYONE ELSE* is doing! It feels good. It does. We have all been there. We have been conditioned to conform and go along with the masses. All our lives we are taught to fall in line, go with the crowd, take a number! Like we are sheep! In fact, that's what it is. We have been living like a bunch of sheep. Just following the masses around. Not even bothering to question what the hell we are doing.

There is this picture that shows a herd of 300-400 sheep being moved through this small gate in a pasture. Ok, yeah that seems normal, but what isn't normal is the fact that there is not even a fence attached to the gate! It's just a gate! Meaning that they are not confined inside at all. They are all just following the others. Doing what all the other sheep are doing. Not an ounce of awareness that there is another way of doing something.

Now yes, I understand that these are animals that do not have the capability of reasoning (that I know of), but is it that far off from the way we live? Just following everyone else around like sheep. Adopting the way everyone else is doing things and calling that our path? That's a life? And while sheep might not have the capability to care what the other sheep think about them, we live in a constant reality where we feel if we do not follow the herd, then there will be some sort of weird repercussion from those decisions. We fear what the other sheep might say, or how they might look at us, or we will be judged for the actions we take for our path. Ok, look, I get it...at some point in our lives, it does feel good to fit in. It does. To be with the "in" crowd, or whatever you call it. We all have this inner desire to be liked. But at what cost? The cost of not aligning with our true self? Our higher self? The cost of not being on your consciously chosen path?

No, thank you. I don't know about you, but that's a hefty cost for me. I am willing to pay this price of stepping out of the conformity and culture we live to create my own way. My way is not one that sets out to appease the masses, my friends, or even my parents.

Ah, now there is something we can all relate to. How many times have we done something to make our parents happy? Too many too count, I'm sure. And look, we all want to make our parents proud of us, but I think somewhere in the mix of all of this we got it confused. Now the way I was raised, my parents were not on the level of making me do things just because that's the way they thought I should be living. Sure, in a protective, loving, stay out of danger, make smart decisions, type of parenting, Yes, but when it came to a certain point in my early adult life (17 and up) they let me make my own decisions.

My mother has always been heard saying; "I just want you to be happy." And it's true. I have made some interesting life choices that led me down some paths I rather have not journeyed down, but sometimes we gotta learn the hard way.

Now, how many of us out there are still trying to make our parents happy? Making decisions on the way that *they* want us to live, what *they* think is right for us, what *they* did? Them is not us. Their path is not our path. We can have an amazing relationship with our parents, but we need not make every decision based on whether or not mommy or daddy will approve. I use those terms in that manner because honestly that's how it should feel to you if you are basing your adulthood decisions on their opinions. Look, we have all suffered from this at one time or another. And I get it. But a lot of people are making HUGE decisions that really are not even their own. Like buying houses, having babies, getting married, going to college, and full disclosure, I am guilty of all of these things. I was so conditioned and under the spell of other people's opinions and just like a good little sheep, I followed in the footsteps of others. Doing the same exact thing. FUCK! What was I thinking? Well I wasn't (FYI- I have no children but was oh so close). And I did all these things under the influence of other people's thinking and motives, not my own. Just because I wanted to fit in and truly, and honestly I feared what others might think or say if I didn't go along with the perceived master plan. Now I am not saying to go full rebel, outlaw, lost boy. Or maybe I am. You must be able to put aside what people are going to think of you and feel about what YOU are doing and what YOU want to do.

The way I see it is like this, what other people think and feel about me is NONE OF MY BUSINESS.

I ask you to adopt this. I ask you to let this really sink into your subconscious mind. Get emotionally involved with this beautiful notion. Carry it around, daily. Because it's true. Let *them* carry around what they think of you, let them harbor the feelings they have. No need to even investigate it. Because if you have really tuned into the principles that have been laid out for you so far, you must have some good people around you. People that can accept you for who you are and what you would like yourself to represent in this life.

We must stop trying to impress others. You must start by impressing yourself first. I no longer seek outside recognition or seek to be congratulated by others. I do the things I do now to impress myself first, and if other people enjoy my work and my craft then that's just a bonus to my situation. We expend too much energy giving a fuck about what others are impressed by. I say, and I encourage you to, to transmute and channel that energy into your own conscious and chosen path. Put that energy, you are simply wasting to good use into projects and passions that make you come alive! What do you think this book is? I could give a fuck less about what others thought of me when they got wind of my writing, dreams, and direction in this life. It is mine!

No one else's! You cannot live someone else's path. So why do we continuously allow people to choose what path *we* are on? Again, this is what you are doing when you...

Give a fuck.

Look, people are going to talk shit no matter what you do. It is just a fact of the world we live in. People will criticize from every angle. Trust me, people do not realize that criticizing is just confirming the fact that they do not have the guts to do something themselves that they desire to do. Think about this, it takes a lot more guts to encourage than to criticize, and that's why most people want to involve themselves in the latter. So, why not be doing something that lights up your life? Why not be doing something that fills your days with passion, joy, abundance, and allows you to thrive in a constant state of happiness? Stop trying to understand why people feel the way they do about you. It is simply a waste.

To end this rant and principle, I am telling you that you can only hold up this façade for so long. And what happens after you figure out that the life you have been leading and the decisions, actions, and behaviors that have been running your daily life have been someone else's? What happens? Complete unhappiness. That's what. And as of late, we have all been exposed to this by the impact that social media has played in our lives. It's a complete competition and comparison game. It's not all bad. Social media can be used as such a great tool, if you choose to utilize it in that manner. But it can also become a dangerous game of trying to be like everyone else and letting *influencers* tell you how to live. Ask yourself this, what are they influencing you to do? What type of influence are you under right this very second because of social media? As I write this, I have recently taken a break from it. A detox if you will. It is needed. Even though I use social media as a tool for my messages and to spread awareness of the information and education I would like to share, I needed it.

Understand this. You are on your own timeline, my friend. Please do not compare your chapter one to someone else's chapter twenty. Take your time and choose your own path. Never mind what everyone else is doing. Do your own thing. Choose what is in harmony with your soul. With your path. With your timeline. Choose your own creative expression. Find your own niche. Be that fucking unicorn that you know you are. The world needs more of them. That's why I am driven to share like I do. To wake up the collective consciousness here on this earth to be able to raise the vibrational level of the world. I am doing my part. Start doing yours by leading your own life, living in your own flow, expressing your true self, and by not giving a fuck. But first...

*"You will never reach your destination if you stop
to throw stones at every dog who barks."*
-Winston Churchill

Key Points To Remember

Stop Giving a Fuck Challenge

Please list 3 things that you have been holding back or in because of what others might think and say.

_____

_____

_____

*Now....please list the **worst** case scenario for each of these things that if you acted on would happen. Confront them. Write it out. Play them out in your head and in this exercise. I promise It's not as scary as it sounds.*

_____

_____

_____

Principle 6

"Stop Procrastinating"

I am going to hit you with something. Yep, some more brutal truth. There is no perfect timing. If you are under the spell of the belief that there is some sort of magical time to do something, then I am here to tell you that you are heading down the path that *many* take that encourages you to NEVER start. Waiting. It's a waiting that will never end. I have always possessed this type of mindset. Until I figured out that I was the one who can create the perfect timing. You do not have to wait on the right circumstance; you can create it for yourself, and when I shifted to this perspective and belief, my life shifted. I was compelled to just fucking do it.

Let me repeat that again. YOU, yes YOU, can create the timing. YOU are the one that creates the circumstances in your life. You are not a *victim* of circumstance you are the *creator* of it.

Got it?

But isn't that an exciting notion to involve yourself with? At any moment in your life you can decide to go down a new path. You can use the available resources that many of us neglect, or think that we do not have access to in order to get started. But you do. We all do. Especially in this age. Everything is at a push of a button. Literally thousands of resources are available to you for FREE! Hell, even my last book I released for free, and if you haven't read *How to Solve the Square Root of Your Problems,* then I suggest you do.

It doesn't matter your current circumstances, whatever you can do in this present moment...act on it... NOW no matter what it is. Take a step in that direction. It does not have to be leaps daily, but it can be small steps to get you to wherever it is that you're going.

Most of us allow our current situation to hinder us from starting anything. We are attached to the notion that because we haven't done these things in the past, we cannot do them now. We use past experiences of life as a basis to determine whether something is possible or not possible for us, and this is a dangerous game to play. Just because you haven't achieved something up until now does not mean you cannot start down that direction and end up achieving it. It's true. But if you never go out and take a risk, you will never know. You automatically fail. You lose. You forfeit. Failure is just a state of mind. In my opinion, it doesn't even exist. Let me explain, pal.

Everything is an opportunity. An opportunity to learn and to grow. To be better, to use it and apply it for your future self to be able to kick-ass. I am sure that you've heard of all sorts of successful people falling flat on their face, only to use that situation or opportunity to learn from it and to be better next time, and ultimately succeeding in whatever endeavor they set out to achieve. You can do the same, but if you never try and you sit around and wait on it, you will be in the position of waiting forever.

I initially moved out to Hawaii to be part of a nutritional start-up. Now obviously, since you're reading about this, the idea did not play out. At least not for me, but the guy who had the idea in the first place had said something to me over the phone when we first started hashing out ideas of the platform of the business, etc. Now at the time I was living in Cape Coral, FL. I had moved there after my second divorce to clear my headspace and to start going down a new path. Anyways, he stated: "I have been waiting on the right people." Now when I heard this, it did not register with me at all. Just the idea of moving out to Hawaii to start a new business was just too exciting for me to notice the red flags. But again, he stated that he had been *waiting*. Well what if we had never reconnected? What if I never showed up? Then what? I will tell you what, he would've been waiting forever, and to my knowledge he still is. After I left, I haven't heard a peep from this business we started. Nothing! I suppose he is waiting around again. Actually, I know he is. I ran into him at a restaurant and I casually asked him if he was still pursuing the business he had been wanting to start for some time. Can you guess his response? Yep. He stated that he was waiting to find the right people and investors. What?! Still waiting? For what? This dude will, in fact, be waiting forever. What the fuck is the wait for? And I asked this so bluntly because most of us have this type of mindset when it comes to doing things we might want to pursue or achieve. I want to ask you something, surprise!

What exactly are you waiting for? Name some things that you think will need to align for you to start this project or endeavor? Please. Really list them. Now, after you have listed these things I want you to take a long hard look at them and answer this: Are these things *really* hindering you from starting or are they just glorified excuses that allow you to continue putting it off?

This saying is something I have really been a fan of: **Make adjustments not excuses.**

BOOM! It is true.

Most of the time we are not really diving into these excuses and allowing them to stop us from getting started. Just start making adjustments in your life so you will open up the availability for you to get on with it. Now, I am not sure of what you are wanting to start, there could be a list of a million things that we all desire to do. But come on now! You can make some steps in that direction. It doesn't have to be *one giant leap for mankind* stuff, it can be little steps.

Even moving an inch moves you closer. Do not think in totalities. Break it down. If you can make some type of move in that direction every day, then you are winning!

Earl Nightingale stated that anyone that is on course towards the fulfillment of a goal is successful. So get on course! Get successful. You are not only successful when you have reached your goal, you are considered successful when you know where you are headed and are taking action to fulfill the desire (more on goals in Principle 9). You can plot out the course by taking small steps daily in the direction of said goal. That's it! Waiting and staying in the same place day in and day out, and always talking about it isn't going to move you any closer. I did this for years when it came to competitive bodybuilding. I talked about it for years. I desired to compete, to go through the mental toughness it took to prepare for a show, I wanted to do it so badly, but all I did for years was talk. I talked about it. I was always procrastinating. Never moving in the direction of achieving it. And by the way, why did you think I put the previous principle (Stop Giving a Fuck) before this one? Because once you stop giving a fuck what will people will say or do, it makes it that much easier to start moving!

I finally decided that no matter what I was going to do this. I started to think of how I could start moving in that direction. I started to plot a course for myself. I broke it down into action steps. I figured out what I needed to do in order to get there, and then I made adjustments in my life in order to do so.

Re-read the previous paragraph. What did I do? What did I finally do?

I decided.

You must decide. Make a fucking decision. Anything! Anything will be better than sitting and waiting for something. There is one common theme in all the books that I read on self-help, success, and personal development and that is the ability to make a decision, and to make it quickly. It is said that successful people decide quickly and make changes slowly, if any at all. And unsuccessful people are slow to decide and change it often. Remember the "every action is a vote for the type of person you want to be" quote? Yeah, well think of this as one of those votes. What kind of person are you voting for with the inability to decide on something for yourself? Marinate on it.

Oftentimes we have amazing ideas, but the fact that we do not make a decision to act on them slowly causes that idea to fade, and then the energy, which was behind that, pushing it your way, is now gone, and then you are just waiting around again. Decide! Not just on ideas that could honestly change our entire life, but with anything.

Life is going to pass either way. Time will keep on ticking as you sit and wait for something to happen. Whatever that may be for you.

I state this again so your subconscious will start to pick it up.

You are a creator. I promise you are. Create the circumstance for yourself. No amount of waiting will build any kind of life you desire or goal you set out to achieve. How you ask? No worries, I explain it all in the next principle.

"A man who procrastinates in his choosing will inevitably have his choice made for him by circumstance."
-Hunter S. Thompson

Key Points To Remember

Stop Procrastinating Challenge

Please list 1 or more thing(s) that you have been thinking about and wanting to do but have made every excuse to not start.

_____

_____

_____

List 1 or more excuse(s) that you have been giving to this desire and start to analyze it and come up with at least one adjustment that could be made in order to get started.

_____

_____

_____

Principle 7

"Set Some Damn Goals"

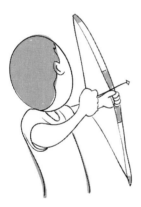

Let me ask you. What are you doing with your days? Are you in a cyclical lifestyle where everyday is like Bill Murray in *Groundhog Day?* Acting out the same situation over and over and over? Going through the motions of life, just sleepwalking through life and safely to our death? How can this be rewarding in any way? Let me mention this before we go on...Same ol', Same ol'. I HATE that saying! When I hear people use this phrase, it honestly makes me want to shake them and shake the dust off of their brain and yell, WAKE THE FUCK UP! Truly. It gets me! It does! Do we need to go back and visit Principle 3? Watch Your Mouth?

OK...hold on...Whew...

Now that I've calmed down we can continue. Is this how you really perceive your life? Same ol'? Same ol'? Same old what? That's a fuck of a way to describe your place here. That is no way (in my educated opinion) to describe this beautiful existence that has been given to us. We are capable of so much more, but most of us are undershooting. We are aiming so low that it's quite embarrassing if you can really take a long hard look at the situation. And I say situation in the manner of our culture, society, and how most of us are living and being brainwashed into thinking we are less than. We are brainwashed into this belief that there is some order in which to do things in life and that's all there is. Wake up, go to work, live for the weekend, and not to mention complain all weekend about what you do all week, only to find yourself getting up and doing that shit year after year. Living for the two weeks (maybe) you get from vacation. Hating Mondays, stuck in a box, going to another box on wheels, and then to the box you live in. We live our life in boxes. We live like we have forever, but we don't, pal. I mentioned this earlier, we get one shot at this thing.

So why, in the name of sweet baby Jesus, do we continue to *not* do anything about it? We just go on about our days hoping and wishing something might come along and save us. We wait for death. We wait for it, but we are already dead. Yeah dude. Dead.

I believe that it was Helen Keller who said "Life is a daring adventure or nothing." And I agree with the lady! I didn't always though. I thought that I was living and creating a life, but all I was doing was managing one. Most of us are. We are not consciously creating a life that we can be proud of, we are managing a life that someone designed for us. All I was after was a good job. Gee, if I could only get a good job and enough money to get a nice car, a house, be stuck under someone's watch all day, just to hit the repeat button over and over?

AHHHHHHHHHHHHHHH!!!!! No! Never again. I couldn't do it. I always knew there was something about me jumping around from job to job, trying to find something that I fully, honestly enjoyed, and would do for free! I never found it. Now, I have had some jobs that were amazing in my time. I worked for Google for nearly two years on a contract, and that was some fun and interesting times. I met some amazing people, learned from some great leaders, and was given an opportunity as a leader myself. Awesome job, really it was, but it wasn't what I really wanted to do. I can, however, tell you it was comfortable. Really comfortable. Worked from home, made a nice paycheck, I was able to travel each month if I wanted to, rental car allowance, per diem. I'm telling you it was comfortable, baby! So yes, lets speak about that word.

Comfortable. Most of us are in this comfort zone. Some of us might not even know that we are in it, but we have been there for a long time. I am not denying it's a nice place to be. It's oh so nice. But it's also a dangerous spot to be in. When you are that comfortable and you are provided for with some cushy perks, it's nice to stay there. It's warm, cozy, and it's familiar. Most think if I have shelter, clothes, food on the table, then I am in good shape. And look, I'm not denying that this is bad to have. But is that all we can really strive for? Is that it? Really? Come on now. Most of us are completely comfortable receiving inferior results. You *know* you are better than that. Like something was telling me that I denied for so long, that I could be doing better. Something that really fires me up. Something that makes me not able to wait to wake up and do it all over again! Waking up and saying let's fuck shit up. Hahaha! Can you honestly say what you are doing for a living is what you *really* want to be doing? Is that what you have always dreamed of? Are you living out your passion? Are you fully expressing yourself in some way? Are you creating a life or managing one?

How can one create a life full of joy, self-discovery, and adventure?

Ok, here is another question for you: what would you be doing with your days if money didn't exist? Go ahead, answer it. If you cannot, you might want to figure that out, or else you are going to be working for someone, doing something that you don't want to do for the rest of your life, and creating a whole heap of lower vibrational feelings that only bring with them not so welcomed outcomes for your reality. Facts. What would I be doing? This. Writing and expressing myself. Do you think when I started to write this book, I had any funding to do so? Was there anyone paying me to do this? No. I don't have a publisher, and no I did not receive an advance (yet), but I continued to write this. Because it's one of the channels of expression for myself. The other was creating content in the form of video messages on my IG. If you follow me then you know all about those. I receive no payment for those, but I continue to release one almost every other day. Oh, and another thing I currently do, and have no interest in ever stopping is my podcast show. I don't get paid for that either. In fact, I pay for that service. I also pay for my website, I pay to self-publish and release my own books. I already have one book that I self-funded to create, design, advertise, and release, and you know what? I gave it away! For FREE! That's what type of passion I have with this industry. That's how much I believe in it. That's where I found my fire! This is the kind of stuff I involve myself in, daily. Regardless of the outcome of money. I truly believe that when you pour yourself into something that resonates to the core of your being that the abundance will follow. Whatever energy you're going to be putting out will always, by law, come back to you, and when it does make its way back to you, it will be tenfold. It's a law. Look it up.

This stuff lights me up. I absolutely love what I do with my days.

It's time, my young grasshopper, to set some goals. Yep, goals. Setting goals around this type of adventure and creating an action plan that will support reaching said goals will have you vibrating on a different level and will cause you to be moved into action. Not only for which endeavor you intend to embark on, but remember in Principle 1? Where we discussed the four departments of life? We must set goals for each of the departments along our way.

You see, the true gift lies inside the person you must become in order to reach the goals you set for yourself. In whatever that may be. I recently heard that each action you make is like voting for the type of person you want to become. It's true. Take that notion into this goal setting adventure you are about to take. When you start setting goals, you will have to eliminate some self-defeating behaviors. Ones that are hindering you from reaching the goals you set. Like if you want to lose weight and set a goal of losing twenty pounds, what type of activities or decisions will you have to refrain from in order to reach the goal you set? That's why Principle 1 is so important. You must be able to identify what is keeping you from living a better life. What type of things are you currently acting out daily are keeping you from hitting that goal.

I wrote this book in a precise order. Each Principle working off the next, each building from the previous. By the time you finish this and the exercises in it, you will have another sense of direction for your life and equipped with more awareness and perspective to not SUCK!

Now in the last couple of paragraphs I am not telling you that you need to quit your job you currently have in order to be happy--or maybe I am, I'm not sure-- that's for you to find out. But setting goals outside of what you are currently doing will add so much more life to you and the ones that you love. We feel best when we are working towards something. Remember the *Groundhog Day* reference? How can that be considered a full life? It simply cannot. Admit it, you feel your best when you are consistently achieving something. Anything. We can encompass the feeling of being at an all-time high in life when we are progressing. Moving towards something. Yet, we tend to not think of it like this. We don't understand that after being in the same type of cycle year after year, that this is in fact what is wearing us down and making us feel like complete shit because we haven't progressed. Your mind is a goal-striving mechanism, baby! We need to constantly give it an aim. Something to shoot for. What are you shooting for? How can you be shooting for something if a target is not present in your life? What is your target? I always have several targets. All of this works off of one another. I am always striving to achieve something. I have found out that I do feel amazing and at my best when I continue to work at something. Small daily things and all the up to writing this book.

Understand this: you are giving yourself goals whether you know it or not. Do you realize what type of unconscious goals you have been setting? Don't you think that it would be a lot wiser to set up precise goals and to plot an exact course of action for your goal striving mechanism to work off? And to hit?! Yes, of course!

I compare this to a boat set out to sea. Imagine this boat having no captain, no course plotted, and no visible plan in place? Sure, it might bump into *something* with some dumb luck and eventually reach something, but wouldn't you rather have a boat that had a conscious captain, an exact course plotted, and visible plans written out on how to get there? Sure, it might get off course occasionally, but it will get to where it's going with direct intent, and it will be exactly where it wants to be, and not on some strange land that you really did not want to end up on.

Does this make sense?

Well, this is exactly what we are doing when we stroll through life with no set plans or direction, or no goals in sight in order to allow us to reach our desire or our own beautiful island paradise. We must continue to set up goals for ourselves in order to progress and to thrive! We are the only creatures on this beautiful planet that does not reach our full potential. We are. Nothing else on this earth does the same thing as we do. Every other creature reaches their full potential, unconscious of it or not. It is true.We get content, we get comfortable, we set no goals for ourselves, and we end up living a life that we are unhappy with.

Wow, that is some depressing shit, but it is true. We must grow and reach for more in order to feel our best. We are born creators, so go create! Set some goals up for yourself. Start thinking about where you really want to go and who you really want to be. Get serious about it. Don't be that boat out to sea with no destination plotted or no plan of action. Be the boat that knows where it's going, and yeah, you might get knocked off course sometimes, but that's why the next Principle is so important to understand when you start moving in another direction. You will need to do this next step daily.

"Goal setting is powerful because it provides focus. It shapes our dreams. It gives us the ability to hone in on the exact actions we need to perform to achieve everything we desire in life."
- Jim Rohn

Key Points To Remember

Set Some Damn Goals Challenge

Please list 3 small goals that you would like to achieve within the next 30 days (choose whatever you want).

_____

_____

_____

Please list some action steps you will need to take, using the available resources, to start moving in the direction of the achievement of these goals?

_____

_____

_____

How will you monitor your progress?

_____

_____

_____

Principle 8

"Use your power of Imagination/ Visualization....properly"

When was the last time you used your imagination? Let me rephrase that question: when was the last time you used your imagination for the benefit of your well-being? You see, all of us use our imagination daily. But, in most cases, it is for the wrong reasons.

You can put your imagination to use in two ways: Worry or Faith.

Most of us are using the first and neglecting the latter. We consistently use our imagination to create the worst-case scenario for ourselves in most situations we encounter. Why is that? Why do we tend to lean towards the worst-case scenario for ourselves by imagining it happening? It's like wishing and hoping for those things to happen. We are *asking* for what we do not want by doing this. Thoughts do truly become things.

Ok, quick lesson, and it's from the Bible. Now, I am no theologian, far from it, but in my studies, I have found that there are many lessons in the Bible that apply to the notion of how powerful your mind is and can be. When it is properly used, it can benefit every department of your life. In Proverbs, Chapter 23, Verse 7 it states, "As a man thinketh in his heart, so is he." Now what does this mean? It means that the thoughts that you become emotionally attached to and hold in your mind, will manifest into your reality. Those thoughts, being anything, will come to pass.

Believe it or not your thoughts are a powerful source of energy, my friend. They are. James Allen wrote an entire book based on this theory. Or should I say FACT. It is called, *As a Man Thinketh*. Allen opens the book with this statement:

> *Mind is the Master power that molds and makes,*
> *And Man is Mind, and evermore he takes*
> *The tool of Thought, and, shaping what he wills,*
> *Brings forth a thousand joys, a thousand ills: —*
> *He thinks in secret, and it comes to pass:*
> *Environment is but his looking-glass.*

Read it again. And again. Until it really sinks in. Really grasp and understand this concept. What you think about all day you become, and in the sense of imagining what could go wrong, or right, you are putting power out into this Quantum Universe. And at some point, these thoughts, if emotionally attached with (in your heart) will manifest in the form of people, opportunities, lessons, experience, and ultimately shape your reality....giving you *exactly* what you ask for.

By asking I really mean thinking. What do you think the power of prayer is? Most of us are praying for what we do not want. Prayer is thought. Prayer is asking. And the first step of receiving is what? Asking.

So, what are you asking for with the thoughts that you hold in your mind. What type of life are you asking for with the things that you think about all day? We *become* the thoughts that we meditate on all day. Sinking in yet? I sure as hell hope so. If you resonate with *any* of these principles I have laid out in this book, let it be this one. This might be the most powerful one. Honestly, I think it is.

Most of us continue to display ignorance by not really understanding this notion. Most of us are trying to change our behavior when the root cause of the continued self-defeating behavior is the fact that we are not seeing ourselves in this image. We continually think about ourselves in a negative manner, which will then manifest into a negative environment and results.

If you can never imagine or visualize yourself with achieving something then it will never happen. But when you allow yourself to focus and use the act of visual/imagination properly on something, and continually visualize the thing that you are, then it will become so.

It has been said that the average human has between 50,000 and 70,000 thoughts per day. Whoa. And it is also said that an overwhelming percentage of those thoughts are negative. Yeesh! It is in your best interest to use your thoughts wisely. It is in your best interest and honestly everyones around you that you become more aware of how and what you are thinking about all day long. I think we can stop here and talk about awareness a bit. Look, this entire book is made to raise your level of awareness. The entire premise of this book was written to introduce thought-provoking ideas that, honestly, have been around for some time.

I am just spilling it back to you in my own words, and unique delivery of the message. It is all here to raise your level of awareness. I believe that better awareness can allow us to make better decisions, which will lead to better results. The more aware we are of what is going on inside of us the better we can understand ourselves and others, which will in return allow us to have a clear vision of what the hell we are doing. Cultivating better awareness for ourselves is key. Awareness of the thoughts that drive us into taking massive action or drive us into a corner seeking safety.

Before we move on, let's get clear on this idea. You are NOT your thoughts. You are the receptor and the channel in which thoughts flow to and through you. It is up to you which ones you attach to yourself and give meaning to. I think for most of us we think we are our thoughts. And I know we have all had moments in our life when we have had some type of wild and crazy thought pass through our mind that made us say, "Where the hell did that come from?" Now, that wasn't necessarily *your* thought. Remember thoughts are energy, and energy is in a constant state of movement/vibration, never being created or destroyed. So, what is happening is that you are *tuning* in to a thought. You are tuning in to that certain frequency, and the problem for most is that we take ownership of whatever comes into our domes and we run with it. We emotionally attach ourselves to it, which then puts us in a certain state and moves us into action, backed by the thought that wasn't even ours to begin with. Now, I am not saying that all thoughts aren't ours. You are a creator. You 100% create thought, but not all that pass to and through you are actually *yours*. This is where awareness comes in. This is where you need to get smart and really decide on which ones you want to agree with and which ones you let resonate in your creative and subconscious mind.

Here is a story that happened to me recently that will prove that thoughts are truly energy and not only that, but powerful as fuck. Currently writing this part of the book I am living in Hawaii, on the island of Oahu. I live right outside of downtown Honolulu. Honestly, to even read that line is still surreal to me, but this is where my path has landed me, and I am nowhere near sad about it. I am truly blessed. Ok, so anyways, the point is is that I have been bartending at a small grill and bar (who shall remain nameless), and it has allowed me to put a lot of cash flow into my endeavors, which I am grateful for. Now I consistently share the fact that I also work while I grind on my side hustle. I think it is inspiring for other people to say, "Hey, you can still work and start something on the side, you have the time," until eventually, your side hustle will gain more and more momentum until you can be financially independent doing what you love. And doing what fills your life with an overflow of passion and abundance; ok, I swear I am getting there.

I worked with a girl, Brittany, and she is really trying her best to get on her path. Her old conditioning, like most of ours, is strong. She moved out here about four months ago after her fiancé passed away from a drug overdose. I mean dude, she is twenty-four. That's heavy and a pretty brutal event to take place in someone's life. Her mother came out here with her and left and let her be on her own. So, for now, she is basically flying solo in an unknown land. Trust me, I know the feeling. But nevertheless, we have chatted most nights we have worked together, and I offer my advice and guidance that she seems to be really letting sink into her subconscious. She consistently takes the bus or walks home or even takes Uber, which you know can put a dent in your budget. Today when I was taking a stroll to my nearby gym, a thought shot across my mind like a bolt of lightning and it was, "Give Brittany your bike." I had the ability, and immediately it resonated with me. So, I texted her a couple of hours later and told her that I was offering her my bike and that I would not take no for an answer. She texted me back extremely grateful and we had a nice exchange of words. I told her that I was coming to our work to hand her the key to the lock because I had left it there the night before.

When I arrived there and after she showed me even more appreciation with a great big hug, she thought it was the craziest thing that I randomly texted her and offered her my bike. She said a couple of hours before I texted her telling her the good news, her and her mother had been talking about getting her a bike and she was thinking about receiving one, CRAZY! That "thought" that her and her mother shared, I was able to tune into the frequency of I received it through the channel of my walking organic antenna (trust me, we will go into this further in the next principle). Now, to me, that is some powerful shit.

I feel like since I have been on my path, that giving has been one of the single most powerful things you can do for yourself and someone else. Everyone wins. Honestly, I have heard it called the most selfish thing that you can do because it makes you feel so good when you do it, but doing it from a sincere place instead of from a place of what you will receive in return reshapes the power of it. There is a saying out here that goes "If can." If I can, then I will. So, I truly believe I have been tuned into the frequency of giving, and what happened on that day proved to me that I was on the right path and am getting more clarity and getting signals a lot clearer for the benefit of not only me but others.

I just wanted to share that story with about thought and how truly powerful your thoughts can be. And the fact is the day before this whole situation I started to write out this principle and I was stuck on how to finish and when that happened the very next day, I knew it all aligned for a reason. It was so cool how it worked out, which proves once more the fact that I desired to finish this chapter of the book and my thoughts manifested a situation for me to practice what I am speaking to. So, get aligned with some good thoughts. Whatever you hold dominate all day will show up in your reality. I promise you.

So be mindful of your thoughts my friends.

Now I leave you with these *thoughts*.

Thoughts can manifest for you. Thoughts are energy. Thoughts are frequency. Thoughts are powerful. You are not your thoughts. You can tune into thoughts.

"Thoughts become things. If you can see it in your mind, you will hold it in your hand."
-Bob Proctor

Key Points To Remember

Use Your Imagination/Visualization Properly Challenge

Visualize something that you would like to align with in your life.

Write it out here. Start with:

*I am so happy now that*_____

_____

_____

_____

Read this daily upon awakening and right before you go to sleep. When you read this, imagine yourself as already having it in your life. Put yourself into a relaxed state and think about how it would feel to have it. Practice this technique for a minimum of 5 minutes daily for 30 days. Watch what changes take place and how you will be moved into action to make this happen for yourself.

_____

_____

_____

Principle 9

"You Cannot Do Awesome Things If You Don't Feel Awesome"

The previous principle is a powerful one to marinate on. Trust me, but this principle goes hand in hand with it. In fact, no matter how many good thoughts you can hold in your mind, it will not matter one single bit until you can put yourself in the proper state so you can actually FEEL awesome.

It is not only what you think, it's what you feel. It's not *all* thought based. Its feelings. Vibration of thoughts and feelings. You keep hearing me say "emotionally attached," and this is what I mean. You must feel not only think. You must put your body into a good state in order to vibrate at a higher level and watch all yourself align with your highest good.

You must be able to feel good.

So, how do we feel good, Zac?

Well, the first thing we need to do is get your vehicle (body) feeling good. In my first book I talk about the power of movement. Movement equaling exercise. This should be a no brainer. It really should. I firmly believe in the notion that if you don't use it you will lose it. We must cultivate the ability to move our body each day and you need to find your own flow of doing so. There are a million modalities out there that can absolutely help you tune in to your health. Whether it's yoga, crossfit, bodybuilding, triathlons, hiking, swimming, mountain biking, pilates, running, rock climbing, etc., you can find out what works best for you so you can create a healthy habit of moving your body and staying in shape. Most people think it's about vanity, and yes, we can completely become body focused where all we put energy and focus into is looking good.

Understand this...

Looking good is a byproduct of being healthy, but it's not about getting six pack abs, (although that would be awesome, it's not the goal) it's about feeling good. It's about being able to be mobile when you're in the later years of your life. You cannot and will not be able to achieve amazing things in your life if you continuously feel like shit. Period. The most prescribed medication from doctors is the same across the board, pal...DIET and EXERCISE! Although it's probably the last thing that you want to hear, it's true. It all goes back to cultivating the habit of doing it. If you haven't been exercising for quite some time, yes, it will be absolutely miserable getting back into it, BUT, if you take your time and set some goals around it and not focus on the macro of it and break it down into micro habits that you can install into your daily routine, you can and will get "there" in time. Start slow and start small.

I believe in taking a holistic approach to healing yourself and movement of the body daily is at the forefront of it all. It's how I start my day, everyday! No questions asked. And yes, it is easy for me because I have such a deeply ingrained habit of doing it, but that came with time. Now it's just part of what I do. Movement of the body first thing in the morning does a multitude of things for you and your body.

Exercise reduces levels of the body's stress hormones, such as cortisol. It also stimulates the production of endorphins, chemicals in the brain that are the body's natural painkillers and mood elevators. Lower stress you say? I'm in! I mean that should be enough reason right there for you to install a morning habit of exercising. Low stress? Sign me the fuck up.

Exercise neurochemically releases natural mood elevators. I mean, come on, dude. That's good news, yes? Still not buying it? Ok, The release of endorphins will trigger a positive effect in your body similar to morphine! Facts…look it up, it's worth a Google, I promise. This will absolutely combat that little bastard known as depression. Don't believe me? Give it a shot. I double dog dare you.

It is said that twenty to thirty minutes of exercise, while endorphins are being released, will result in an energy and mood boost for two to three hours and a mild buzz for twenty-four hours. Buzz? Who doesn't want to be buzzed all day? Naturally! Still not buying in? Ever heard of the neurotransmitters known as Serotonin, Dopamine, and Norepinephrine? These are all known to be linked to depression and having an imbalance of these can cause types of depression in the body and mind, but when exercising regularly these are all released in an abundance. Imagine if you are exercising on the regular. Do you think this might have some type of positive effect on your overall well-being? YES! Yes it will. Now you can get boosts of all of these neurotransmitters in other ways. That's for damn sure; however, the most healthy way is through exercising, sweating, and moving your damn body. A common misconception of energy is that you can store energy or save it. No, no, no. It's like "Let me rest so I can feel more energized." This is completely backwards. The more you are lazy and lay around like a slob the more tired you will be. It's like sleeping for twelve hours thinking that you will wake up feeling more energized because of all that rest. No, dude, you'll just wake up even more tired. The more active you are the more energized you feel. You can tune into an infinite amount of energy. I swear it. But first you need to tune your body up.

It's not only exercise that is going to get us there. Although it is a huge part of this equation. We must have a nutrient dense diet feeding and fueling our bodies on the daily. Garbage in, garbage out. I mean, we can all tell the difference in how we feel when we eat a big, fat greasy burger (although they are oh so delicious) compared to when we eat a nice whole meal of lean meat, complex carbohydrates, and leafy greens. There is absolutely no comparison. Now, I am not going to sit here and preach about what "diet" you should tune into. Every-BODY is different. There has been an ongoing debate about what people should eat to feel the best, and that is for YOU, and YOU alone to figure out. What is going to be sustainable for you? What is going to make you feel the best? What will keep you lean and feeling energized throughout the day so you can be at your absolute best? For me, it's whole foods. Now we talked about the 80/20 rule earlier in the book, and I also apply it to this. 80% of the time I am eating whole foods that are sustainable, and 20% of my day I will have some junk, protein bar, cereal, whatever. I am not trying to tyrannize myself in any manner, but what I am trying to achieve is a healthy relationship with myself and my intake of food. That's my goal. A loving, healthy relationship with foods. Not being too indulgent and also not being too strict. This will only lead to binge eating, starving yourself, and developing some type of eating disorder that will have you in a bad spot quickly. So educating yourself, learning about what works best for you is key. But I think we can all agree that what I stated earlier is what it's all about: Garage in, garbage out. It's what I've been preaching this whole time. You cannot expect to get positive results when you continuously put negative things in. It can't work, pal. Start tuning into your nutrition. Ask yourself: is this going to make me feel good? Is this going to keep me healthy? When we can gain an awareness, and create a habit of eating well 80% of the time, when we go to eat that 20% of garbage we will not shame ourselves all day, we will actually enjoy it and keep moving on.

No need to tyrannize yourself. It will not go well, I promise, I have been there.

When you combine a healthy diet and implement an exercise routine into your life, things will shift for you. Your mood will be elevated, you will have the ability to tune into an infinite amount of energy, your sleep will improve, your confidence will sky rocket, you will add some years to your life, and you will inspire others around you to do the same. Everyone wins.

When you start feeling awesome, you will start doing some awesome things.

"Health is a matter of choice, not a mystery of chance."
-Aristotle

Key Points To Remember

You Cannot Do Awesome Things If You Don't Feel Awesome Challenge

What are 3 things you will immediately implement to start creating a healthier lifestyle for yourself?

_____

_____

_____

What are 3 emotionally charged reasons for you to create a healthier lifestyle?

_____

_____

_____

Principle 10

"Learn How to Be Alone & Filter Out Distractions"

I have become very partial to my solitude over the last few years. As you might have picked up earlier, I have been married twice, both being pretty much back to back. I met my second wife about 3 weeks after the first marriage ended. That was where I was at. I mean do you think that I was in a mental space to jump right back into a relationship after four years of being with someone? I was not seeing as clear as I now wish I had been, but I can understand the immense amount of lessons that I can take from the situation I had allowed myself to get into. If I were to have possessed the outlook I have today, then I would've taken some time off, but then again, would I be the person I am today?

Hmmm. That's for another book.

I highly suggest looking into gaining some more solitude in your life. There is always so much noise around us all day, every day! Especially nowadays. Most of the time we are pouring ourselves into things for others. We are quick to do something so we will not let someone else down, but what about letting ourselves down? I think that we constantly do this when we do not have enough "me" time. Don't get me wrong, I believe that it's great doing for others, but what is your limit? What is your boundary? When do we shift the mindset that it's going to be beneficial to everyone when more "me" time comes into play?

I think a lot of us are stuck in this type of mindset. We don't have enough "me" time. And that time is necessary for internal growth. You absolutely need some personal space in order to be at an *all-time optimal performing level.* If you can achieve this type of state (which is doable) think about how much more effective you will be for the close ones who surround your life. First be a badass for you so you can be a badass for others. Everyone wins. You must first make it a priority to have some time. The old "you can't pour from an empty cup" saying. It is true, trust me. The more energized you are the more energy you have to put back into projects, loved ones, passions, and whatever else you involve yourself in. Everything you touch will turn to gold. This is how you give back more. The more you give, tenfold is returned to you. Believe me. You will be in a *peak state*. I believe this comes from self-love practices and the ability to focus. Which means filtering out the distractions.

But first you must start with giving back to you. Self-care is a form of self-love, and that, my friends, is a form of self-respect. It all comes full circle when you go down this path. Treat *you* better so others will benefit. That's pretty damn cool if you ask me. This is not selfish rather self-less! Again, the more you can give back to you, others will not only benefit by how you interact with them, but they will be inspired to do the same when they see you beaming and constantly in a state of happiness. How? Well my first book (yes, I know I keep plugging it, but hey it's free) outlines an entire morning routine and the benefits that spawn from this practice. There are tons of books written on it, all in their special way but all have the common theme. Install a morning routine in your life. The first thing in the morning your brain is operating straight out of theta into alpha waves, which means this is the time when you are the most impressionable.

So, make sure you're impressing some good, positive things on it! And what better time to give back to you when you are most impressionable? This is where your days begin, and those days become weeks, and the weeks, blah, blah, blah. You get where I am going with this. It becomes your life. So the ol' "I don't have time to give back to myself routine," isn't going to work this time. We can all carve out some time for ourselves in the morning. Even if it does mean getting up a little bit earlier than you are used too. Challenge yourself. Remember when I mentioned earlier that every action and decision you make is like voting for the type of person you want to be. Well here it is, hero.

This is where you can really let that sink in. What type of person will you need to be by being in a peak state? A person that feels his best. What type of person feels their best? One who gives back to themselves. How would that person give back to themselves? By treating themselves well. How would that person treat themselves well? By taking care of the mind, body, and spirit by installing a morning routine for themselves that gives back to each department of life. That's what type of votes you will want to be casting. Be that person. This is also the best time to have zero distractions; with zero distractions present and pouring yourself into something that fully gives back to each part of your well-being, you are only setting yourself up for an extremely successful day and life! The self-care practices that one can install in the morning will have a lasting quality that will carry you through your days.

One BIG self-care practice I firmly believe in and will give you all the "me" time that you desire and really need is meditation. I have been practicing meditation for a few years now. I love it. I do it first thing in the morning. It has always given me lasting benefits throughout my day as well by helping me to stay centered, gain more awareness, and to really tune into my own inner voice or intuition. Yeah, it's in there, and if you can quiet the distractions down in your life and give a listen to what *you* are saying, you may be very well surprised. And that's why meditation is such an enormously helpful practice to install in your life. Especially in that block of time in the morning where you are the most impressionable.

In my opinion, to have a successful meditation practice, a few things are required. One, you will need to be alone, which covers the solitude part. You must find a quiet, comfortable spot that you enjoy, which covers the self-care/love part. Think of one spot that makes you feel like it's your own little hideaway, one that you would like to retreat to, maybe when you are having a challenging day. Think about that place for *you* for a minute. What feelings arise from thinking of this nice, cozy personal spot?

Ok, good, remember those feelings when you are going to meditate, this will only help put you in a more relaxed state. When we are relaxed, we feel good, we are vibrating on a certain level that makes us feel a certain way that enhances our mood and well-being, hence why it falls under the self-care/love part of this whole principle. Meditation will also require you to clear your mind and quiet the noise in your head, block out distractions, and fully and completely allow you to be in your own space. It. Is. Amazing. It hits ALL the points I am stressing to you in this principle. Start now. Even if it is just five minutes per day. That's a great start. I, personally, listen to ambient sounds, frequencies, and tones set to be in tune with our own resonance. This helps me to tune in on another level. You can find a plethora of these sounds on YouTube. Plus, there are a million apps readily available for you to download to assist you in fully owning this new practice.

Before we move on, I would like to dive into distractions. Our life is so very full of distractions. I mean they are everywhere if you really start to analyze your daily activities, which you have already done right? Considering you read Principle 1 and stepping the fuck out of your own way to see what the hell it is that you're doing. Also, Principle 7 Set Some Damn Goals. By applying these principles, you will have a *kung-fu ninja grip* type grasp on what is distracting you. A lot of us tend to let ourselves be bogged down with distractions all day long. Pulling us further and further away from our true selves and path. Distraction leads to dilution, which may make you end up walking around like a zombie, distracted all day and never focusing on what it is you need to be doing to not suck.

Can you think of some things that are distracting you from moving forward? First think about it. Now, go ahead and identify three things in your life that you KNOW are distracting you.

1.

2.

3.

That wasn't so hard was it?

And one thing before we proceed:

Do your very best not to passively read this book and skip over the challenges. They are here to help you to gain some new awareness, better understand of yourself, and to identify some things in your life that are self-defeating and very well the cause of your misalignment. So, I ask that you really involve yourself in the exercises. Writing it out is powerful and a good way to really plant that new seed of positivity into your subconscious.

We must be able to identify what is distracting us. And look, I am all about a good time, I am! But the things that seem to be distracting to us tend to be the more pleasurable things. In a physical sense.

Reminder: We are very physical creatures but understand that the biggest part of us is non-physical. I have attached myself to the belief that I will be casual about things that are distracting me from my highest self and not habitual about them. If you are getting distracted by choice that is one thing. If you are constantly distracted out of habit, then think twice, pal. Video games, tv, social media, porn, sports, etc., are among the most distracting of shit you can find. It's not serving you, I promise. Its just bullshit to keep you stupid, distracted, and diluted down.

Ready for some stats? I thought you would be! Recent studies show that the average amount of time someone watches TV per day is between four to six hours daily. What. The. Fuck. I was one of these zombies for quite some time. Now, understand that I still do watch TV, but only by complete choice. And it's for the sole purpose that I want to be in a mindless state. Usually after I have been working for hours or doing something where I'm really flexing my mental faculties.

I vividly remember that's all my second wife and I did most nights; TV, Halo Top, no communication, and completely engulfed in the programming. Because that's what it is! It's the ultimate distraction. It is programming you on all levels! And I wonder why my marriage suffered. If we had spent half of the time working on cultivating ourselves and our relationship with one another, it might've been a different story and a different book, but I am not scared to admit I have poured mindless hours allowing myself to be distracted by this one thing. It was a great time, it was, but so self-defeating on so many levels. I read stats like that and paired with the overused excuse (might I add) that "I don't have enough time," yeah, you do!

Imagine if you took two of those hours and applied it to doing something that will lift your spirits, help to cultivate a better relationship with you and your loved ones, and maybe even make you some money. I highly encourage you to put one of those hours at the beginning of your day by installing a morning routine that puts you in a great state and one that will help you to see and receive all the gorgeous blessings and opportunities throughout your day, and then you can take the other hour and apply it to maybe a side hustle, working on your relationship, an online course, or giving back to your community. And that's just two of your hours! You can still have two to watch whatever is trending on Netflix at the moment.

Folks, that's only the TV statistics...shall I dive into the stats on social media? How much screen time are we using? It is said that the average time a person spends on social media is two hours a day! Shit! Pair that with TV watching and hell! That's a part-time job! That's between six and eight hours being blindly distracted! YIKES! Have we even thought about this? How much time do we really give to these self-defeating distractions?

Do we think about how much energy is being put into things that are not going to have us aligned with our true selves and not even close to helping us reach our full potential?

People!

Listen to this now. This must be stopped. We are turning into zombies.

That's why I have been going in on this principle. We must be able to give back to us. We must be able to get in tune with our own frequency, not on the frequency of all this artificial bullshit. In order to do that it is going to require some solitude, the ability to focus, and the installation of some self-care/love practices.

I am not telling you to completely shut down all social media and watching TV, no. Who the hell am I? I use social media like crazy to build my business and market myself. And much too often I must check myself and take breaks from it, but at least start moving in the direction of cutting down the time used for distracting and empty activities. Create the ability to exercise discipline around the things that are distracting you. Allocate some time for other things. Use your energy wisely. Use your time wisely. You are not getting it back. As grim as that sounds, it's true. Invest your time wisely. It's not the most sought-after commodity on this earth. Time. Not money.

Money comes and goes. It's always there. But time, time is something that once it's gone, it's gone. So next time you feel like involving yourself in things that aren't so great for your mental, physical, spiritual, and emotional well-being, ask yourself what *could* you be doing with this precious time that you have here? That's where my philosophy comes in about being casual and not habitual with things that aren't so great. But hey, occasionally, it feels good to fuck off. Just don't make it a daily ritual.

After all, we are having a human experience, so why the hell not get into some bullshit every now and then? I get it man, I do, but what is going to be more important when the day is over? Getting distracted and involving yourself in shit that is only going to be self-defeating, or having the ability to shift your behaviors and actions to more beneficial ones? Gain that awareness to consciously *choose* when and where you will let yourself get into a little bit of bullshit.

It's a split. I've been consistently running a 80/20 split for my life. 80% on top of my shit, grinding, doing the work, focused in, progressing, etc., and 20% complete bullshit. It feels better to me, especially when I'm in the 20%. It feels better because of the split. I can enjoy the bullshit *more*, because I am putting *more* of the work in. So when I go to eat the pizza, or binge watch some Netflix, or stay in bed until 9am, it feels so much better than doing that 80% of the time.

We've all seen *The Shining*...well we've at least heard of it, hopefully. There is a scene in there where Jack Nicholson, who plays a writer that has taken his family to a closed/seasonal hotel to write his next book, and he is basically losing his shit, and he types out a multitude of pages that state:

"All work and no play makes Jack a dull boy."

It's a proverb, and it's true. You gotta have the balance. But although we need a balance, we have to stay aware if it is a healthy balance. Is your balance 80% purpose and 20% pleasure? Or the other way around? We NEED to keep this in check. Always. Look at your split. How does it measure out? And if you can't answer that question, then take a look at your current results in life and then I promise you will have that answer.

Purpose > Pleasure.

"I live in that solitude which is painful in youth, but delicious in the years of maturity."
-Albert Einstein

Key Points To Remember

Learn How to Be Alone & Filter Out Distractions

What are some things you can do to create some solitude in your life? How and when will you implement these things?

_____

_____

_____

What are 3 distractions you can start to work on so you can gain more focus on your life?

_____

_____

_____

Principle 11

"Take Time Out of the Equation, It's Already Yours"

I briefly mentioned this notion earlier, but it is vital when it comes to living out your life in a joyous state. And of course, not sucking. I believe that most of our misalignment in this life and the fact that we might stay a little bit more frustrated than "normal" is the fact that life is not happening the way we think it *should* be happening. Facts. Truth bomb. BOOM.

When you start moving in another direction or towards something you desire, you must have a relaxed attitude about it. As previously mentioned, if you use your imagination in the form of worrying, how it's going to happen or when it will happen, when all you are doing is pushing it further away? It would be like you were forcing it to happen. What typically happens when we force things? It doesn't feel right and it usually isn't right, which means it probably won't go right. We must try our best to cultivate a relaxed state of mind in the pursuit of something better for ourselves. If we do not have the ability to make ourselves feel good, how far do you think those thoughts are going to go? Yes, they are powerful but without the necessary energy or emotionally charged feeling, it most likely will not happen for you. The more centered and calm we can go about our pursuits, the better. That's all I am really trying to say here. I could end this principle here, but if you know me, I have a challenging time shutting up.

Think about this: all you could ever want or be, you already have and are. Read that again.

It's true. As I have mentioned earlier, you have this power already inside of you. All of it. But worrying about it or putting an end date on things will only leave you standing in a position of lack, and when we stand in a position of lack, the vibrational state we put ourselves in will only attract the things that will push us further away from aligning with our true potential. It WILL happen for you. Whatever THAT is for you. And what's your rush anyway? It's absolutely none of your business how or when you might align with whatever reality you are trying to meet. That's the universe, baby. YOUR job is to let yourself AND the universe know that you're serious about it. Now yes, everything you could be you already are, but you must take the necessary action in order to align with that person. You must move through some layers by taking the action and tapping back into that true potential you've been ignoring for god knows how many years. It's all in the act. I know we have all heard the expression: "Act as if." And yes, I do agree with it, but only to some extent. Whoever you're trying to tap back into, whoever and whatever that highest version of yourself looks like, what would that person be doing? What type of habits do they have? What type of goals have they set? How are they looking towards the future? And then when you can answer these basics, you have some actions to take.

Want to know the best way to progress on a consistent basis? *Incremental Progression.* We tend to want to bite off more than we can chew when we are out to pursue something. We tend to look at the totality of it. We want to go after the main course right off the rip. We want to skip the breadsticks, but my advice to you is to start with the breadsticks. Don't go after the main course right off the rip. Start slow. This is the best way to ensure success, build the muscle for bigger goals, and slowly start to build self-confidence and self-worth. It's completely ok to start slow. Take time out of the equation. If you take time completely out of the equation you CAN'T NOT get there! It is inevitable. You are on no one's timeline but your own. Here is a catchy quote to go with that last line: "Comparison is the thief of joy." For sure it is. Go at your own pace. I promise you are not "behind." Behind who? NO ONE! Know this: one step forward is better than where you are at right now. Just one. If you could get 1% better every other week, you'd be 26% better in a year! And 52% the next, and so on. And the results will stick! They will stick more than you getting to wherever you're going real fast. And I promise you it is not the way you want it. Instant gratification might sound good, but I can tell you from a massive amount of experience, when you work hard at something and you stay steady grinding, and let nothing get in your way it feels fucking beautiful, baby! Most of us want the results now. We want a quick fix for life. We want it all now. And in the current cultural climate I don't blame you, dude. But slow, small steps will get you there. They will compound. If you can adopt an attitude of having delayed gratification, shit will start to shift for you. That's what successful people do. They sacrifice the present for the future. And they stay in the space of patience. Patience is truly a motherfucking virtue my friend. The art of practicing patience is a challenge to master, but you do not get good at something without ever doing it. You gotta start and you gotta start small.

Sidenote: oftentimes when we are not patient and we get that "something" we thought we wanted then often we realize that it's not what we really wanted in the first place.

Don't dive into ANY of this information at once. Whether it's practicing patience, moving towards your goals, distancing yourself from friends, getting brutally honest with yourself, or learning to be alone. Just start small, baby! You will "arrive." And you never truly "arrive." Remember that self-mastery is life long. When you get to one point, it's time to move to the next, and then the next, and then the next. Be on a consistent level-up and enjoy this crazy journey/process of life.

"Your future is not ahead of you, it's inside of you."
-Dr. Myle Monroe

Key Points To Remember

Take Time Out of the Equation, It's Already Yours Challenge

What is something that you have been wanting to align with in your life?

_____

_____

_____

What has ever made you think or feel that you couldn't achieve it or it wasn't already yours? Is that your belief or something you have emotionally adopted as your own? What could you do to change that belief?

_____

_____

_____

Principle 12

"Forever be a Student"

As I mentioned earlier, human beings are the only creatures on earth that do not grow into their full potential. Although we have the capability and power to do so, we neglect to cultivate our true, innate potential. Now why is that? If we have the capability and the power to do so, why don't we? I think one reason is pure fucking laziness. Yeah, that's one reason, for sure. At one point did you accept the belief that you were done growing as a person? When? Tell me! (just kidding) But seriously, when was it that YOU decided to stop reaching your full potential?

If you are not growing, you are what? In a very harsh way, you are ultimately dying. I recently heard someone say as I passed by them: "I am 27 years old, I'm not trying to learn anything new." Needless to say that when I heard this my head exploded! Do you know how dangerous this thought process can be if you decide to adopt it? Most of us, myself included for some time, thinks that as we grow older that we are done learning. Once traditional school is over then we are officially done with it...

What. The. Fuck?

Look, if you really want to go down that road, give this a proper think: if you decide to stop learning, expanding your consciousness, pushing your mental limits, challenging your current beliefs, then you will forever be stuck in the same exact spot you are in, forever. And by "spot," I mean in all areas of life.

Not too sure about you, but to me, that sounds God awful. We are meant to grow as humans. We are not human beings, we are human becomings. Your growth journey is never over! You can always learn more, challenge yourself, and push your limits. Speaking of that, how do you even know where your limits are if you are not consistently pushing them, and actually exploring where they are? How will you ever know how far you can go, or who you can actually become in this life? Not to mention all the people you could potentially inspire by doing it.

Speaking of people. I stand firm in the fact that you can learn from everybody! Yes tis' true. I promise. Look at it this way, you can either learn what to do or what not to do. So be open to interactions with everyone (within reason). Why? Because you never know if the next interaction or experience you have with another person will change your life. Sound dramatic? It is. But it's true. I've heard things told to me and I could hear someone else say it in a totally different way and it clicks. That's why I listen to so many speakers and lectures. I never know when something will jump out at me and could totally course correct my life.

I mean damn! Self-mastery is life-long people. I have attached myself firmly to the belief that you could always be more, learn more, do more, reach higher, and go further. I think it is fun to see how far I can go. I have gotten to the point that I am really never satisfied. Now, let me take a moment and explain myself, I am happy where I am at, and you must be. You cannot get from unhappy here to happy there. It just doesn't work like that. Content but never satisfied. That's the attitude I carry these days. I always find myself challenging and pushing me to be better. We are truly our own worst critics, but you can always step back and recognize where you were and how far you have come. And enjoy those moments. Take the time to self-reflect and know how much of a badass you truly are and then turn it the fuck up! Do more. The next level of you is always going to require a different version of you. Whoever you were to get to this point, is not going to be the person that gets you to the next level. And I think that even though it is sometimes an overwhelming thing to think about, it's also very exciting.

By doing the work and by work I mean the inner work, you constantly change and broaden your perspective of life. You change the view for yourself. The view looks a little different from a squirrel to an eagle. Why not rise? Why not fly high? Why not reach your fullest potential in life? Aren't you even just a little bit curious about what your life would look like if you reached a place where the views and your external reality would shift for you? What could it be? What would it look like? Who would be there? Who would you be? Who would you align with?

Before I close this principle out, let us take some time to think about the marketplace. We can all relate to this. By marketplace I mean the job marketplace. I used to always wonder why I couldn't get, or for that matter, keep a high paying job. I went thirty-four fucking years never really building any type of skills for myself so I could be more valuable or provide more value in the marketplace. I was pretty steady with jobs throughout my life and I could never quite grasp the fact that I wasn't learning anything new.

I worked some great jobs. I worked for Verizon Wireless, State Farm, LifeTime Fitness, and the all powerful, Google. And I made some pretty good money. But it was like I was hitting a ceiling with my income. Why? The value I brought to the marketplace was shit. I mean look, I was a damn good salesman, but I never learned more, I never read, I never took a course, I never listened to the lectures, went to the seminars, sought out a mentor, or joined a mastermind. So my value stayed the same, and I always ended up with the same type of income. But as soon as I realized what I needed to do I hit the fucking ground running. And everything that I mentioned above that I wasn't doing, I started to do. All of it. Even joined Toastmasters to be a more effective speaker and communicator, and within three years I increased my income by over 10x!!! And maybe this isn't the classiest move, but I want to be as candid as I can with you.

When my life was at an all time low and I had just separated from my second wife, I was working at Steve Madden making $16 per hour at thirty-four years old. Not exactly a great memory on my highlight reel of life, but it's where I was and I am cool with that. Because as I look back, I was only in that position because I had stopped learning. I poured so much into myself and built the ever loving shit for value in myself. I was a relentless outlaw, an unstoppable rebel force with it. I found something that I was absolutely fascinated with and wanted to pour my energy into and I learned every damn thing I could about it. And as I sit here and type this I still continue to pour all the knowledge I can into my mental factory on a daily basis.

So, anyways, I went from making $16 per hour to $180 per hour. Correct. You read that right. Over 10x my income. It took me three years, but hell man, if someone told you that you could multiply your income by 10x in three years would you waste any time starting to go down that road? 10x baby! Why? Because I built the skill set and value in myself, and I had become that valuable in the marketplace. I went from selling shoes to being the Vice President and Chief Operating Officer at an Experiential Therapeutic Youth Center, and while this book has taken several months to write, as you can imagine, my life has changed quite dramatically. This chapter is being written all the while my business partner and I have opened the doors to that very place ten weeks ago. It's surreal to even be typing this out, but I sit here to tell you, speaking my most authentic truth to you that you can do the exact same. Maybe not open a youth center, but anything that you find a passion for or want to become a master at. Learn everything you can about it. Now it's not all about the money and there are several different ways to define success or growth, but I think we can all agree that money seems to always be a hot topic in most of our lives. And think about how learning and growing and expanding your consciousness can do for all other areas of your life, not just the financial. Your mental, spiritual, emotional, and even physical departments. As you learn, build, and grow all of these areas will grow with you. Allowing you to reach your absolute highest potential.

I encourage the fuck out of you to start learning. Educate yourself and find your own flow with it. We have unlimited resources of information at our fingertips. Use it. And then go apply it. Knowledge isn't power, it's only the beginning of it. Adopt the knowledge and then take massive action in applying it to your life. Use what you learn and watch everything in your life change.

"If money is your hope for independence you will never have it. The only real security a person will have in this world is a reserve of knowledge, experience, and ability."
-Henry Ford

Key Points To Remember

Forever be a Student Challenge

List 3 things you can do to start building more value into yourself.

_____

_____

_____

List what those 3 things will bring into your life when you start to apply them.

_____

_____

_____

Principle 13

"Be Vulnerable"

It seems that most of us are under the impression that showing your true feelings is weak. Crying is weak. My second wife once told me that men shouldn't cry...come again? So, just because I am a man I cannot show emotion? And you know what? During the time of our marriage, I didn't cry. I involved myself so deeply in that belief system that I adopted and accepted it. NUTS! CRAZY! As I have stated earlier, we are emotional creatures. We should be feeling all emotions. Not just sitting in them, but allowing them to be felt. We should be allowing them to flow to and through us, learning from them, understanding them, to better understand ourselves. Guy...girl...it's ok to cry.

Showing your authentic self is beautiful and empowering. Having an emotional release is amazing. Never let someone tell you anything different. If they do, they might be having challenges being their authentic self. An emotional release clears out energy. Energy that has been more than likely pent up inside of you waiting to get out. When we do not allow our true emotions to be released in some manner, we suppress them. Suppression leads to depression, depression leads to disease. Now there are healthy ways and unhealthy ways to release emotions. When we tune into them and become aware, we can respond to them accordingly and find a healthy channel to allow them to flow outward. When we simply react to them and allow them to lead our decisions and actions, and not tune in and become aware of what is triggering us, that's when trouble ensues. It's a practice. The more you do it, the better you will get when recognizing when they surface or when you are triggered by something. And I will say it again: you do not get good at something by never doing it.

Losing your temper is weakness, loss of control is weakness. You become powerless to that. You're handing over your power to that emotion or that person. Harnessing your emotion and learning from it and channeling it in a positive manner is power. That's true power. Power isn't "raging" out on someone for pissing you off. Power isn't allowing someone else to control your emotions. That's for you to do. Control and direct that emotion. Learn from it. What is it showing up for? What is it showing you? What could it teach you about you?

That's power.

Power is speaking your truth. Allowing yourself to be vulnerable. Showing vulnerability is strength. We have had it backwards in our culture and society. Most of us grow up with a heavy dose of toxic masculinity or femininity and we stay in that space most of our life. The secret is to integrate them both into your life. That is power. It's a challenge, I know, but it's how we are built. We are conditioned from an early age to think that we have to be one or the other. To combine both of these into our lives is the way we are meant to live. It's beautiful when done properly. And look, I do not have it figured out completely, but I stay aware when either side is taking the reins a little too much. It's a blend, and you have to find your own flow. That's why it is so vital to allow emotions to flow into your life. All of them. But when shining your light of love on all of them, they are only going to allow you to reach your highest self and potential. Think about how effective you would be in every relationship in your life if you could integrate both of these energies into your life. You would be a better co-worker, partner, son, daughter, wife, mother, husband, father, student, lover...human. Does this make sense? Man, I am on a good ramble on this Principle. That's ok though. If you have made it this far, you have tuned into how I write. I allow myself to be shown. I am vulnerable. I am acting in my most authentic energy and that's what it's really all about. Be you, dude. Just be you. It's ok. You're amazing. You're a beautiful soul and the whole world should see who you really are. At your "worst" or at your "best" let them all see you for you. Be vulnerable. When you are able to do this, you are also allowing everyone around you to do the same thing, how cool is that? Cry, speak your truth, set healthy boundaries for yourself, be bold. Let someone know how you feel, tell them what's on your mind, don't hold back.

Want to know another secret? None of us are making it out alive. So why not let the world see who you really are in every light. Good, bad, ugly. You can get much further by being you. You're unique. There is no one else like you on this earth, I promise you that. Stop trying to be someone else, everyone is already taken. Show yourself.

"Vulnerability is not winning or losing; it's having the courage to show up and be seen when we have no control over the outcome. Vulnerability is not weakness; it's our greatest measure of courage."
-Brene Brown

Key Points To Remember

Be Vulnerable Challenge

What steps are you going to take in the next 30 days to be more vulnerable?

_____

_____

_____

How will you reflect on the steps you have taken?

_____

_____

_____

Principle 14

"Don't Pursue Happiness"

Happiness is not the goal and it never should be. Why? Because you are not always going to be happy. Period. You cannot be in a constant state of happiness. If anyone ever told you that you can always be happy, I recommend questioning them. Think about it. Honestly. There is a natural duality to life.

Pleasure → Pain

Happiness → Sadness

Joy → Sorrow

Yin → Yang

Night → Day

You cannot have one of these without the other. But these things are also temporary. Now I'm not saying that you cannot be happy most of your life, because I truly believe that you can. But there will be times in your life when you will feel like shit, angry, sad, annoyed, frustrated, etc., the list goes on, dude.

There will be times in your life when things will happen beyond your control and that is just the nature of life, that is the nature of being. BUT again, these are all temporary. We seem to not fully grasp that notion and truly believe it. All of it is. It's all fleeting. Understand that. Know that. Believe that. We tend to want to sit with these things longer than we should. We want to spend the weekend with our emotions, we want to take them on dates, we want to make them our best friends, take them on camping trips, and vacations. We allow ourselves to sit with these emotions for far longer than we need to, and when we do that they slowly become a part of who we are. That emotion takes over and starts to lead us, it starts to make decisions for us, it starts to talk for us, and then there is the other side of it, which is when you completely try to block these emotions, not allowing yourself to feel them, denying them, and doing your best to not let yourself feel. Understand that by engaging in this behavior will only lead you down a road of self-destruction.

Carl Jung said it best when he said, "What we resist, persists." I absolutely love this quote. What he is articulating is that whatever we try to deny and give our energy to blocking out only grows bigger. Like if I tell you not to think about a blue elephant, don't think about a blue elephant, don't think about a blue elephant...what are you thinking about? A fucking blue elephant. Same thing will happen with your emotions. Whatever you try to not feel will only grow larger within you. If you are not allowing yourself to actually feel these emotions then they will only build up inside of you and the longer they build up on the inside the more toxicity you are allowing into your being. This can be extremely dangerous for your well-being. When we ignore what we truly feel it creates misalignment. By not channeling and releasing emotions we cause build up, which typically leads to us exploding in some manner.

There is definitely a balance somewhere in between allowing yourself to feel emotions that come to you and allowing yourself to suppress them. Find your balance, but do not get good at something by never doing it. It comes with practice, it comes with a better sense of awareness, it comes with being in tune with yourself and the emotions that you feel. Notice the cues when something might trigger you, "good" or " bad." Notice these things and the earlier you can catch them either showing up or staying too long will dictate what type of energy you will have and emit. Happiness is not the goal. No...no...no...Again, we are emotional creatures. I know it is a good day when I feel ALL emotions. When I can truly KNOW what it means to have this human experience and to actually experience and to feel all of it. I promise that the more you practice this, the more you can actually stay in an amazing flow of life. Allow and release. Allow and release. Come on, say it with me...

Allow and Release.

Allow and Release.

Allow and Release.

Allow and Release.

Make this your mantra. At first maybe when you find yourself sitting too long with an emotion you can begin to use it. Emotionally attach yourself to it; it serves as a great reminder of you recognizing what shows up for you and to allow yourself to feel it and then releasing it in a healthy manner through a positive channel.

So, once more for you people in the back. Happiness is not the goal. It is not the pursuit. You will feel ALL emotions ALL the time. Let them come to you, let them teach you, let them guide you to your highest potential.

"Don't pursue happiness, rather design a lifestyle where the byproduct of that lifestyle results in the feeling of happiness."
-Dandapani

I will let you off the hook with this last one.

No Challenge.

No Key Points.

Just gratitude and love.

Thank You.
I hope that this book can serve you in many ways.
-Zac Sweat

References

"1944 State of the Union." *FDR Presidential LIbrary & Museum.* www.fdrlibrary.org/sotu.

Allen, James. *As a Man Thinketh; From Poverty to Power.* Thinking Ink, 2011.

Armstrong, Charlotte. *A Dram of Poison.* ImPress, 1956.

Brown, Brene. *Dare to Lead: Brave Work, Tough Conversations, Whole Hearts.* Random House Large Print Publishing, 2019.

"Dandapani Archives." *Goalcast,* www.goalcast.com/tag/dandapani/.

Dass, Ram. *Be Here Now, Be Here Now, Be Here Now, Here Be Now, Be Nowhere Now: Remember.* Lama Foundation, 1971.

Grant, Richard. *Through the Heart.* Bantam Books, 1992.

Hill, Napoleon. *Think and Grow Rich.* St. Martins Essentials, 2001.

Jung, C. G. et al. *Modern Man in Search of a Soul.* Martino Fine Books, 2017.

Koepke, Daniell, and Thought Catalogue. *Daring to Take up Space.* Thought Catalog Books, 2019.

Lambreth, Clifton, et al. *Ford and the American Dream: Founded on Right Decisions.* Daniel Bradley, 2007.

Wellwood, John. *Toward a Psychology of Awakening Buddhism, Psychotherapy, and the Path of Personal and Spiritual Transformation.* Shambhala, 2002.

Lee, Bruce. *Striking Thoughts: Bruise Lee's Wisdom for Daily Living.*

Nightingale, Earl. *The Strangest Secret: How to Live the Life you Desire.* SImple Truths, and Imprint of Sourcebooks, 2010.

Proctor, Bob, and Greg S. Reid. *Thoughts are Things: Turning Your Ideas into Realities.* Jeremy P. Tarcher/ Penguin, 2015.

Robbins, Tony. *Awaken the Giant Within.* Simon and Schuster LTD, 2017.

Shields, Christopher John. *Aristotle.* Routledge, Taylor & Francis Group, 2014.

Skott-Myhre, Kathleen S.G. "Youth: A Radical Space of Pilgrimage." *Youth Work, Early Education, and Psychology,* 2016, pp. 179-193., doi: 10.1057/9781137480040_10.

Thompson, Hunter S. *Fear and Loathing in Las Vegas: a Savage Journey to the Heart of the American Dream.* Langara College, 2019.